Yellowstone National Park encompasses more than two million acres of wild lands and open spaces where animals like elk, wolves, and bison roam. It's a place where biological, geological, and hydrothermal processes each play a part in shaping a fascinating, and constantly changing, landscape. More than 400 miles of roads and 1,000 miles of trails weave through this spectacular land that has been protected "for the benefit and enjoyment" of people like you since 1872.

Because America's first national park is so vast and filled with such a variety of ecological wonders, the question we hear most often at the visitor centers in Yellowstone National Park is:

"What should I do if I only have one day in Yellowstone?"

WE PRODUCED THIS BOOK TO HELP YOU PLAN A PERFECT DAY IN THE PARK.

To simplify your visit to the park, we gathered the advice of local area experts and park employees to create three classic, sightseeing day trips. Each one contains suggested routes and stops so you see the best of what Yellowstone has to offer in a limited time frame. To get the most out of your trip, we suggest that if you have one day to spend in the park, do Day 1; two days, do Day 1 and Day 2; three days, do Day 1, Day 2, and Day 3.

For those with more than three days in the park, or who would like to spend a day focused on a specific aspect of the park, we created six itineraries based on your interests. Also designed by our panel of expert contributors, these trips are great as either stand-alone excursions or supplemental outings to the day trips.

Modify any trip to suit your needs.

No matter which itinerary you choose to follow, feel free to modify it to suit your needs and interests. Still, we recommend that to get the most of your time in the park, start early or stay late to avoid crowds at popular locations, and for the best chance of viewing wildlife. Also, optimize your day by stopping at visitor centers to pick up trail guides and to learn more about the area, recent wildlife sightings, and predicted geyser eruption times. Remember that whatever amount of time you have in Yellowstone, the beauty of the landscape and the memories of your experience last forever.

Stay safe and help protect Yellowstone National Park.

Please refrain from any of the following activities:

· Willfully remaining near or approaching wildlife, including nesting birds, within any distance that disturbs or displaces the animal (Remain 100 yards from bears and wolves and 25 yards from other wildlife.)

· Traveling off boardwalks or designated trails in hydrothermal areas

· Throwing anything into thermal features

· Swimming in hot springs

· Removing or possessing natural or cultural resources (such as wildflowers, antlers, rocks, and arrowheads)

· Traveling off-road by vehicle or bicycle

· Camping outside of designated areas

· Spotlighting wildlife (viewing with lights)

· Imitating elk calls or using buglers, imitating wolf howls, or playing bird vocalizations

· Using electronic equipment capable of tracking wildlife (Consult 36 CFR and the Superintendent's Compendium posted online at **www.nps.gov/yell** for more information.)

YELLOWSTONE
ASSOCIATION
INSPIRE. EDUCATE. PRESERVE.

This book was produced by the nonprofit Yellowstone Association, who has been the National Park Service's official partner in education in Yellowstone National Park since 1933. Proceeds from your purchase directly benefit education and research in Yellowstone National Park.

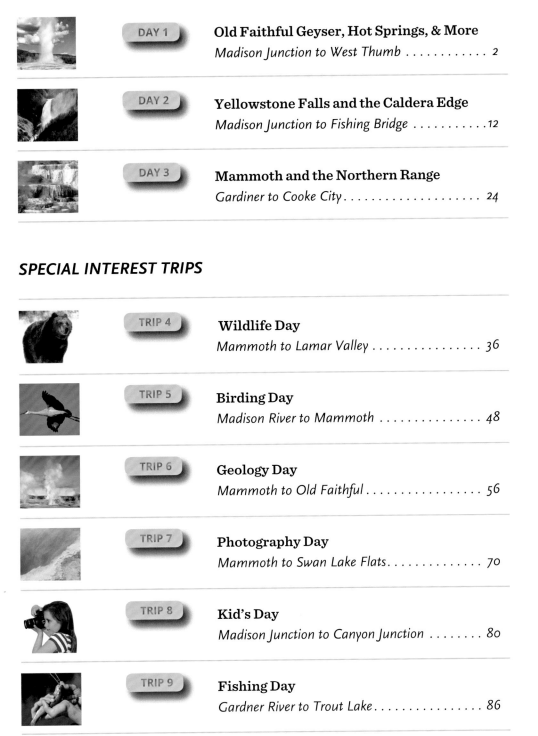

SPECIAL INTEREST TRIPS

Give wildlife a brake. Unless posted slower, top speed throughout the park is 45 mph (73 kph). To assure yourself enough stopping distance if you encounter animals unexpectedly, please slow down.

Watch from pullouts. If you see wildlife while driving, do not stop or impede the safe and free flow of traffic along any portion of the roadway. Instead, find the next established pullout, park, and watch from a safe distance.

Campfires are allowed only in designated grills in park campgrounds, some picnic areas, and specific backcountry campsites. Fires must be extinguished before leaving them unattended. Ask locally about current fire restrictions.

When viewing wildlife, you must stay at least 100 yards (91 m) from bears and wolves. A distance of 25 yards (23 m) is required from bison, elk, and other animals. Regardless of distance, if any animal changes its behavior due to your presence, you are too close.

Do not feed any wild animals, including birds. Consuming human food is unhealthy and encourages aggressive behavior that may require management action. All food, trash, coolers, and cooking tools must be kept secure in a bear-proof container unless in immediate use.

Stay on designated trails and boardwalks. The ground in hydrothermal areas is fragile and thin, and there is scalding water just below. Visitors have fallen through and died here. Keep your children close at hand.

Avoid water hazards. Do not take risks while fishing, wading, or crossing streams. Swimming is unsafe and prohibited in many areas. Park waters can be deceptively cold and swift. All boats and float tubes require permits.

As you enjoy trails, be bear aware. You are safer hiking with groups of three or more. In areas of low visibility, make noise to avoid surprise encounters. Do not run from a bear under any circumstance. Carry bear spray and know how to use it safely.

Control your pet. Pets are not allowed on trails or boardwalks, in the backcountry or hydrothermal basins. Where allowed, pets must be leashed and remain within 100 feet (30.5 m) of a road or parking area. Do not leave a pet unattended or tied to an object. Owners must bag and dispose of pet waste.

Cell phone service may be available in the developed areas at Canyon, Grant, Lake, Mammoth Hot Springs, Old Faithful, Tower, and the North and West entrances. Check with your provider for coverage areas. As a courtesy to others, please silence your cellphone while enjoying Yellowstone's natural features. Wi-Fi is available to visitors at the Mammoth Hotel lounge and the Old Faithful Snow Lodge for a fee.

Old Faithful Geyser, Hot Springs, & More

Madison Junction to West Thumb

One half of the world's hydrothermal features are here at Yellowstone National Park.

Old Faithful, Yellowstone's most famous geyser, is located in the Upper Geyser Basin among many other spectacular geothermal features. Its predictability and impressive display make it the highlight of this trip. This iconic geyser spouts between 4,000 and 8,000 gallons of hot water more than 100 feet into the air every 90 minutes or so. Each eruption lasts between 1 and 5 minutes.

Start the day at Madison Junction and drive south toward Old Faithful. Fine-tune the timeline and stops to fit your schedule and interests. Start early or stay late to avoid crowds, or to see how the light of a sunrise or sunset illuminates the landscape.

Enjoy this tour through some of the park's finest geothermal features.

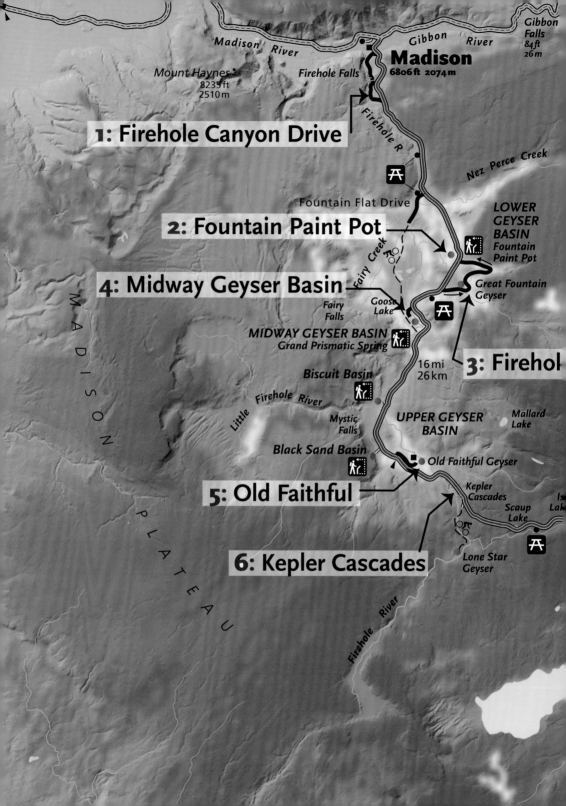

1: Firehole Canyon Drive

2: Fountain Paint Pot

4: Midway Geyser Basin

3: Firehol

5: Old Faithful

6: Kepler Cascades

Madison River

Gibbon River

Gibbon Falls
84 ft
26 m

Mount Haynes
8235 ft
2510 m

Firehole Falls

Madison
6806 ft 2074 m

Firehole R

Nez Perce Creek

Fountain Flat Drive

Fairy Creek

LOWER GEYSER BASIN
Fountain Paint Pot

Great Fountain Geyser

Fairy Falls

Goose Lake

MADISON

MIDWAY GEYSER BASIN
Grand Prismatic Spring

16 mi
26 km

Biscuit Basin

Little Firehole River

Mystic Falls

UPPER GEYSER BASIN

Mallard Lake

Black Sand Basin

Old Faithful Geyser

Kepler Cascades

Scaup Lake

Is Lak

PLATEAU

Lone Star Geyser

Firehole River

HAYDEN VALLEY

CENTRAL PLATEAU

Mary
Lake

Beach
Lake

ake Drive

NTINENTAL DIVIDE

e Lacy
akes

Creek

8391 ft
2558 m

Craig Pass
8262 ft
2518 m

De Lacy

7: West Thumb

WEST
THUMB

West
Thumb

WEST
THUMB
GEYSER
BASIN

HOSHONE LAKE

DAY 1

Madison Junction to West Thumb

- ☐ **1. Firehole Canyon Drive** (15 minutes)

- ☐ **2. Fountain Paint Pot** (45 minutes)

- ☐ **3. Firehole Lake Drive** (30 minutes)

- ☐ **4. Midway Geyser Basin** (45 minutes)

- ☐ **5. Old Faithful Area** (2–4 hours)

- ☐ **6. Kepler Cascades** (15 minutes)

- ☐ **7. West Thumb Geyser Basin** (45 min.)

Photo by Steve Byland, dreamstime

▲1 Firehole Canyon Drive (15 minutes)

This one-way drive follows a portion of the Firehole River. Stop to enjoy views of Firehole Falls and the Cascades.

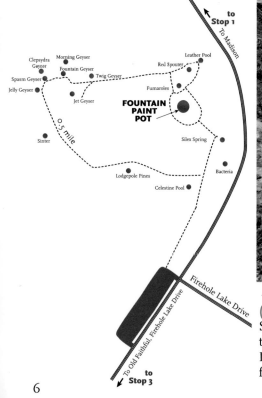

to
Stop 1

To Madison

Leather Pool

Morning Geyser
Clepsydra
Geyser
Fountain Geyser   Red Spouter

Spasm Geyser   Twig Geyser

Jelly Geyser   Fumaroles

Jet Geyser

FOUNTAIN PAINT POT

0.5 mile

Silex Spring

Sinter

Bacteria

Lodgepole Pines

Celestine Pool

Firehole Lake Drive

To Old Faithful, Firehole Lake Drive

to
Stop 3

Photo by jfurik, dreamstime

◀2 Fountain Paint Pot
(45 minutes)

Stop to stretch your legs on this ½-mile loop trail that winds past many hydrothermal features in the Lower Geyser Basin, including Yellowstone's most famous mudpot.

Fun Fact

Does it look like the lodgepole pine snags in this area are wearing white socks? These "bobby sock trees" absorb mineral-rich water that leaves white deposits when it evaporates.

◀**3 Firehole Lake Drive** (30 minutes)
This one-way drive takes you past many geysers and springs, including Great Fountain Geyser, which shoots one of the tallest sprays in the park. Check out the manganese oxide-blackened water of the hot Firehole Lake and enjoy the view of 10,336-foot Mount Holmes to the north.

▼**4 Midway Geyser Basin** (45 minutes)
Walk this ½-mile boardwalk loop to view Excelsior Geyser and the colorful Grand Prismatic Spring (see below).

Photo by Geoffrey Kuchera, dreamstime

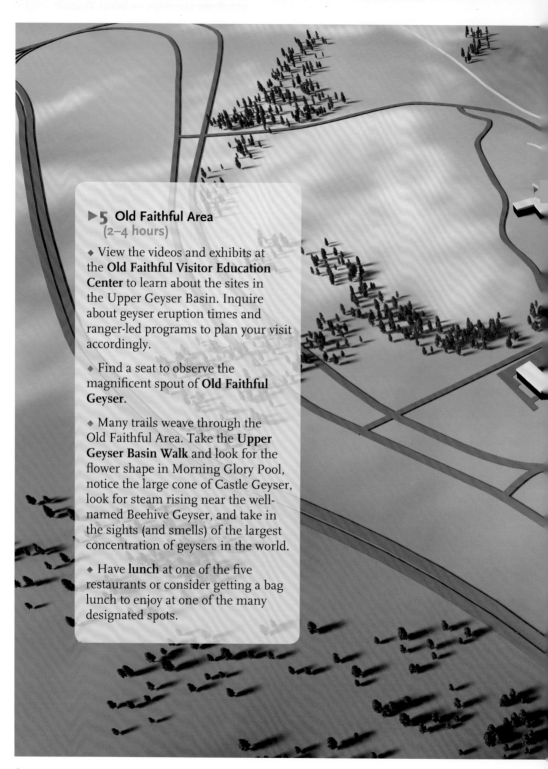

▶5 Old Faithful Area
(2–4 hours)

♦ View the videos and exhibits at the **Old Faithful Visitor Education Center** to learn about the sites in the Upper Geyser Basin. Inquire about geyser eruption times and ranger-led programs to plan your visit accordingly.

♦ Find a seat to observe the magnificent spout of **Old Faithful Geyser.**

♦ Many trails weave through the Old Faithful Area. Take the **Upper Geyser Basin Walk** and look for the flower shape in Morning Glory Pool, notice the large cone of Castle Geyser, look for steam rising near the well-named Beehive Geyser, and take in the sights (and smells) of the largest concentration of geysers in the world.

♦ Have **lunch** at one of the five restaurants or consider getting a bag lunch to enjoy at one of the many designated spots.

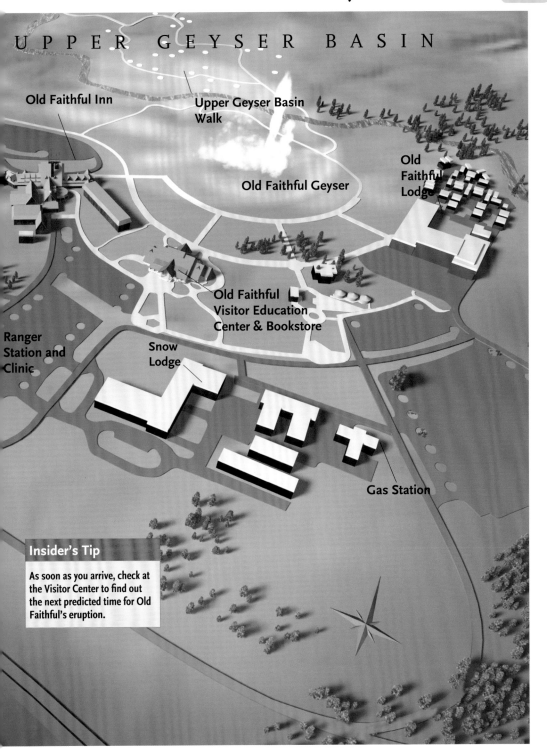

UPPER GEYSER BASIN

Old Faithful Inn

Upper Geyser Basin
Walk

Old
Faithful
Lodge

Old Faithful Geyser

Old Faithful
Visitor Education
Center & Bookstore

Ranger
Station and
Clinic

Snow
Lodge

Gas Station

Insider's Tip

As soon as you arrive, check at
the Visitor Center to find out
the next predicted time for Old
Faithful's eruption.

Photo by Ralf Broskvar, dreamstime

▲6 Kepler Cascades (15 minutes)
Take a short walk to view this series of waterfalls on the Firehole River.

▼7 West Thumb Geyser Basin (45 minutes)
Walk the ½-mile outer boardwalk and ¼-mile inner boardwalk trails to view breathtaking springs and interesting formations, including Fishing Cone, along Yellowstone Lake.

Safety Tip
Be safe. Stay on designated walkways in geothermal areas and maintain your distance from wildlife.

Fishing Cone

Fishing Cone erupted as high as 40 feet regularly in the early 1900s. As Yellowstone Lake's water level rose, the cone was inundated with water, which cooled the geyser so much that it no longer erupts.

Yellowstone Falls and the Caldera Edge

Madison Junction to Fishing Bridge

The dynamic geology of Yellowstone constantly changes the landscape.

Some of the changes, like the rising and sinking of the caldera, happen so slowly we don't see them. Other changes, such as the appearance of hydrothermal features in the Norris Geyser Basin, happen day to day.

A massive volcanic eruption 640,000 years ago formed the Yellowstone Caldera, which is one of the largest known in the world. The caldera sprawls across 1,350 square miles of the park. This trip takes you around and through part of the caldera and past some of the prominent features that have been formed by the ever-shifting terrain, including the Grand Canyon of the Yellowstone River and Yellowstone Lake.

This full-day journey allows you to experience some of the magnificent waterfalls, charismatic wildlife, and wondrous geological features of Yellowstone National Park.

DAY 2

Madison Junction to Fishing Bridge

- ☐ **1. Gibbon Falls** (15 minutes)
- ☐ **2. Artists Paintpots** (1 hour)
- ☐ **3. Norris Geyser Basin** (1.5 hours)
- ☐ **4. Museum of the National Park Ranger** (15 minutes – at the Norris Campground)
- ☐ **5. Virginia Cascade** (15 minutes)
- ☐ **6. Canyon Area** (2–3 hours)
- ☐ **7. Hayden Valley** (1–2 hours)
- ☐ **8. Sulphur Caldron** (15 minutes)
- ☐ **9. Mud Volcano** (45 minutes)
- ☐ **10. Fishing Bridge Area** (1 hour)
- ☐ **11. Yellowstone Lake/ Storm Point Nature Trail** (1–3 hours)

3: Norris Geyser Basin

Norris
7526 ft 2311 m

2: Artists Paintpots

Monument
Geyser Basin
Beryl Spring

Artists
Paintpo

1: Gibbon Falls

Twin
Lakes

Nymph
Lake

Straight Creek

14 mi
23 km

Madison River

Gibbon   River

Gibbon Falls
84 ft
26 m

Madison
6806 ft 2074 m

Firehole R

CONT

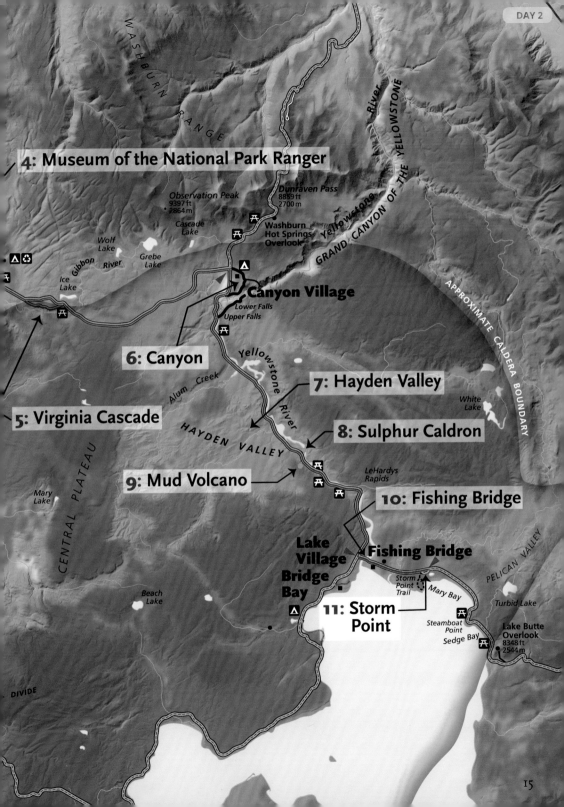

4: Museum of the National Park Ranger

WASHBURN RANGE

Observation Peak
9397 ft
2864 m

Dunraven Pass
8859 ft
2700 m

Cascade Lake

Washburn Hot Springs Overlook

GRAND CANYON OF THE YELLOWSTONE

Yellowstone River

APPROXIMATE CALDERA BOUNDARY

Wolf Lake

Grebe Lake

Gibbon River

Ice Lake

Canyon Village

Lower Falls
Upper Falls

6: Canyon

Yellowstone River

5: Virginia Cascade

Alum Creek

7: Hayden Valley

HAYDEN VALLEY

White Lake

8: Sulphur Caldron

9: Mud Volcano

LeHardys Rapids

10: Fishing Bridge

CENTRAL PLATEAU

Mary Lake

Beach Lake

Lake Village Bridge Bay

Fishing Bridge

Storm Point Trail

Mary Bay

PELICAN VALLEY

11: Storm Point

Steamboat Point

Sedge Bay

Turbid Lake

Lake Butte Overlook
8348 ft
2544 m

DIVIDE

◀1 Gibbon Falls
(15 min.)
While driving along the northwestern edge of the Yellowstone Caldera, take a stop to soak in the scenery and view Gibbon Falls. The Gibbon River tumbles 84 feet over the north-western edge of the immense volcanic crater that formed 640,000 years ago. The short path along the river is handicap accessible and great for people of all ages, including children.

▶3 Norris Geyser Basin
(1.5 hours)
Welcome to one of the most unique places on Earth! Here you are just outside the rim of the Yellowstone Caldera and at the intersection of three fault zones. Features in the Norris Basin spout some of the hottest and most acidic water in the park. Before you begin exploring the basin, stop at the museum, information station, and bookstore to get trail guides and learn more about the area.

Photo by Jason P. Ross, dreamstime

▲2 Artists Paintpots (1 hour)

After driving through Gibbon Canyon, where the river cuts through high walls formed by ancient lava flows, stop for this 1-mile stroll through forest and wetland to view active and colorful mudpots, fumaroles, and springs. Minerals and heat-loving microorganisms create the full spectrum of colors in and around these features. Cool, cloudy days make great photo opportunities.

Insider's Tip

Yellowstone Science, available on the web, is a publication that features articles about research and scientific endeavors in and around the park. http://www.nps.gov/yell/planyourvisit/yellsciweb.htm

Walk the 1½-mile Back Basin loop trail to view the world's tallest hydro-thermal spray, Steamboat Geyser, and Echinus, the world's largest acid-water geyser. The trail also passes a number of colorful springs.

Don't miss the ½-mile Porcelain Basin loop trail. What it lacks in length, it makes up for in the sheer concentration of sights, sounds, and smells.

Photo by Strekoza2, dreamstime

▲4 Museum of the National Park Ranger (15 minutes)

Stop at the museum (at the Norris Campground) to learn about the history of the national parks and the important work of national park rangers throughout the United States.

▲5 Virginia Cascade (15 minutes)

Take this one-way, 3-mile drive along the Gibbon River to view these 60-foot falls, beautiful meadows, and possibly an elusive moose.

Photo by Ron Niebrugge

◀**6 Canyon Area** (2–3 hours)
View the movies and exhibits at the
Canyon Visitor Education Center to learn
about the Grand Canyon of the Yellow-
stone River and the geology of the area.
Join in on some of the ranger-led pro-
grams and pick up a trail guide.
See map on the next page.

▼**7 Hayden Valley** (1–2 hours)
Continue south along the Yellowstone River through glacier-carved Hayden
Valley. As glaciers receded and melted at the end of the last ice age around
14,000 years ago, they left depressions and sediments in the ground that
make this valley so open and marshy.

This valley, named for geologist Dr. Ferdinand Hayden, is geographically,
biologically, and historically significant. It is the heart of the Yellowstone
Plateau and provides habitat for many animals. Artists' renditions from
Hayden's first exploration of Yellowstone in 1871 helped convince the U.S.
government to establish Yellowstone National Park.

Bison, elk, moose, wolves, and grizzly bears often saunter through the
sprawling valley. Marshy areas attract Canada geese, pelicans, sandhill cranes,
trumpeter swans, northern harriers, and many species of ducks. Animals are
most active around sunrise and sunset, so consider visiting the valley early or
late in the day for the best chance to see wildlife.

Stop at pullouts to get a better view of the landscape and learn more about the
area.

Photo by Jason P. Ross, dreamstime

Artist Point

Canyon Area

Yellowstone River

Inspiration Point

Grand View

Lookout

North Rim Loop Road

North Rim Drive (one wa

Take a drive along the **North Rim Loop Road** and stop at the lookouts for some breathtaking views of the canyon. Watch the Yellowstone River plunge 308 feet over Lower Falls from the overlook, or hike to the brink on the short, but very steep, trail.

Canyon Campground

Chittenden Bridge

Uncle Tom's Point

South Rim Drive

Upper Falls of the Yellowstone
(109 feet; 33 meters)

Lower Falls of the Yellowstone
(308 feet; 94 meters)

North Rim Drive (one way)

Grand Loop Road

N

Cross the river at Chittenden Bridge and drive along the South Rim for the best views of the canyon. Stop at Uncle Tom's Point to hear the roar of the river and take pictures of Upper and Crystal Falls. Continue on to Artist Point for spectacular views of Lower Falls.

Canyon Lodge

General Store

Adventure Store

Canyon Visitor Education Center

Norris Canyon Road

Stop 5
Virginia Cascade

Stop 7
Hayden Valley

Photo by Svecchiotti, dreamstime

▲8 Sulphur Caldron (15 minutes)
Stop at this pullout to view this hydrothermal feature, tinted yellow from a combination of sulphur and microorganisms.

Photo by Mirekdemi, dreamstime

◀9 Mud Volcano (45 minutes)
Pick up a trail guide at the parking lot and stretch your legs on this .7-mile loop. Be sure to stay on the boardwalk as you pass this series of boiling and burping mudpots, created by hot, acidic water that softens the surrounding lava rock.

A shorter boardwalk veers north off the main Mud Volcano loop to access Dragon's Mouth Spring. Like many of the park's hydrothermal features, this area is very significant to many of Yellowstone's associated Native American tribes.

Photo by Minyun Zhou, dreamstime

▲10 **Fishing Bridge Area** (1 hour)

View the exhibits at the Fishing Bridge Museum and Visitor Center to learn about the history and animals, especially the birds, of the area. Stop at the store for a drink or snack and then watch fish and other wildlife on foot from the century-old Fishing Bridge. The Yellowstone River flows north here from Yellowstone Lake.

▶11 **Yellowstone Lake and Storm Point** (1–3 hours)

Drive east from Fishing Bridge to explore part of the shoreline of Yellowstone Lake. Watch for geese, herons, ospreys, and other birds while walking through forest and marshland on the short Pelican Creek Nature Trail. Then walk the 2-mile Storm Point Nature Trail loop for sweeping views of the lake. Both lakeside trails are great for children.

Continue to the east and stop at Steamboat Point or Lake Butte Overlook for more lake views. Look for the Tetons in the distance on a clear day.

3 miles east of Fishing Bridge **Stop 11**

Spur road to Pelican Valley Trailhead

Indian pond parking area

to **← Stop 10**

Indian Pond

2.0 mile round trip

Yellowstone Lake

Storm Point

Mammoth and the Northern Range

Gardiner to Cooke City

The Northern Range of Yellowstone National Park is a place of unparalleled wonder and beauty.

Prepare to be amazed by the dynamic hydrothermal features and charismatic wildlife that you will witness on this daylong journey across the park's northeastern corner.

Sedimentary limestone, deposited by an ancient sea, underlies this area. The hot water of Mammoth Hot Springs dissolves the limestone and deposits travertine, forming terraces that shift before your eyes.

This part of the park is home to the highest concentration of mammals in the lower 48 states. The area around the hot springs provides respite for many animals during the long, cold winter months. The sweeping Lamar Valley, with abundant water, forests, and grasslands, also provides prime habitat throughout the year.

The best times to view wildlife are around sunrise and sunset, so plan your day accordingly. Consider starting your day early or ending your day late in the Lamar Valley.

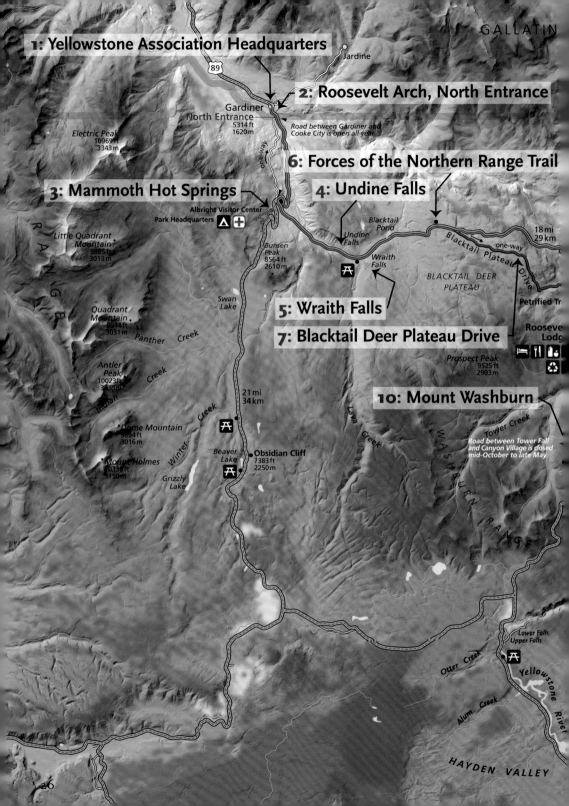

GALLATIN

1: Yellowstone Association Headquarters

Jardine

89

2: Roosevelt Arch, North Entrance

Gardiner
North Entrance
5314 ft
1620 m

*Road between Gardiner and
Cooke City is open all year.*

Electric Peak
10969 ft
3343 m

6: Forces of the Northern Range Trail

3: Mammoth Hot Springs

4: Undine Falls

Albright Visitor Center
Park Headquarters

Blacktail
Pond

18 mi
29 km

Little Quadrant
Mountain
9885 ft
3013 m

Bunsen
Peak
8564 ft
2610 m

Undine
Falls

one-way

Blacktail Plateau Drive

RANGE

Swan
Lake

Wraith
Falls

BLACKTAIL DEER
PLATEAU

Petrified Tr

Quadrant
Mountain
9944 ft
3031 m

Panther   Creek

5: Wraith Falls

7: Blacktail Deer Plateau Drive

Roosevel
Lodge

Antler
Peak
10023 ft
3055 m

Creek

Prospect Peak
9525 ft
2903 m

Indian

Dome Mountain
9894 ft
3016 m

Winter   Creek

21 mi
34 km

10: Mount Washburn

Lava Creek

Tower Creek

*Road between Tower Fall
and Canyon Village is closed
mid-October to late May*

Mount Holmes
10336 ft
3150 m

Beaver
Lake

Obsidian Cliff
7383 ft
2250 m

Grizzly
Lake

WASHBURN   RANGE

Lower Falls
Upper Falls

Otter Creek

Yellowstone   River

Alum. Creek

HAYDEN VALLEY

26

12: Silver Gate & Cooke City

ATIONAL   FOREST

BUFFALO PLATEAU

MONTANA
WYOMING

Slough Creek

Road between Gardiner and
Cooke City is open all year

Northeast Entrance
7365 ft
2245 m

Barronet

Abiathar
Peak
109   m

Tower-
Roosevelt

Slough Creek

8: Calcite Springs Overlook

Pebble Creek

Yellowstone
Association
Institute

Pebble Creek

The
Thunderer
1055 ft
3 17 m

Cache Mountain
9596 ft
2925 m

Tower Fall
132 ft
40 m

LAMAR VALLEY

SPECIMEN RIDGE

Trout Lake

Soda Butte Creek

Cache Creek

9: Tower Fall

29 mi
47 km

Mount
Norris
9936 ft
3028 m

Antelope Creek

11: Lamar Valley

River

GRAND CANYON OF THE YELLOWSTONE

Yellowstone

MIRROR PLATEAU

Photo by Molly Hashimoto, dreamstime

◀1 Yellowstone Association Headquarters, Gardiner, MT (15 minutes)

Start your day with a visit to the Yellowstone Association. Since 1933 the Association has been helping to connect people to the beauty and resources of Yellowstone National Park through education. Take some time to peruse the bookstore, pick up books and maps, and talk to staff to get the latest information on wildlife sightings.

◀2 Roosevelt Arch, North Entrance (15 minutes)

Enter the park through Roosevelt Arch. The arch is named for former President Theodore Roosevelt who laid the cornerstone of this gateway to Yellowstone National Park in 1903. Be sure to read the inscription at the top of the arch.

Photo by Mike Jenkins, dreamstime

■3 Mammoth Hot Springs (2 hours)

• Stop at the Albright Visitor Center to talk with a park ranger and find out about ranger-led programs about this area. Pick up trail guides or inquire about ranger-led walks. Then visit the Yellowstone Association bookstore to shop for an educational book.

• A ⅓-mile paved trail winds through Historic Fort Yellowstone, where soldiers from the U.S. Army lived while administering and working to protect the park after it was established in 1872, through 1918, two years after the creation of the National Park Service.

• Pick up a trail guide and take a 1-mile walk around the Lower Terraces on the paved loop trails and boardwalks to get a close-up view of the impressive terrace formations. When the springs are active, algae and bacteria create a carpet of color beneath the water. When the springs are dry, only the white of the travertine is visible.

• Stop at the Horse Corral parking area for a view up to yellow-hued Canary Spring.

• Turn on the one-way, 1½-mile Upper Terrace Drive loop for a great view of more travertine terraces. These living hydrothermal features change constantly as the flow of mineral-depositing water varies.

• Take the 4-mile, one-way, scenic Old Gardiner Road north back to the main entrance for good views of the surrounding landscape and a chance to see some wildlife.

Insider's Tip

The Heritage & Research Center in Gardiner, MT is home to the park's museum collection, archives, research library, historian, and archeology lab. It houses thousands of historic records, photographic prints and negatives, books and manuscripts, cultural and natural science specimens, archeological artifacts, and plant specimens.
Call (307) 344-2264 to inquire about public tours.

▲4 Undine Falls (15 minutes)

Follow the Grand Loop Road toward Tower-Roosevelt and stop at the Undine Falls viewpoint to see the upper and lower falls of Lava Creek.

■5 Wraith Falls (45 minutes)

Stop and stretch your legs on this 1-mile, round-trip hike through field and forest to view these falls where Lupine Creek cascades 90 feet.

■6 Forces of the Northern Range Trail (20 minutes)

Walk this ½-mile boardwalk and learn about ecological processes in Yellowstone National Park.

■7 Blacktail Deer Plateau Drive (30 minutes)

(Closed at night and in inclement weather)
Veer off the main drive to take this 7-mile winding dirt road into the aspen stands on Blacktail Deer Plateau, through the gorge of Elk Creek, and up Crescent Hill to reconnect with the Grand Loop Road. Watch for wildlife along the way.

◀8 Calcite Springs Overlook (15 minutes)

Pass Tower Junction and stop for this short walk to view the Grand Canyon of the Yellowstone River at its narrowest stretch.

Photo by Alexey Kamenskiy, dreamstime

▼9 Tower Fall (20 minutes)

Stop at the general store for a drink and snack. Then take this 1/3-mile, round-trip walk to the bottom of the 120-foot cascade.

Photo by Julie Lubick, dreamstime

Photo by Matthew Ragen, dreamstime

▲▼10 Mount Washburn (4–6 hours)

If you're up for a rewarding challenge, continue south along the Grand Loop Road to Dunraven Pass and the Mount Washburn Trailhead. The 6-mile, round-trip hike provides some of Yellowstone's most incredible views of the Grand Canyon of the Yellowstone, Hayden Valley, and Yellowstone Lake. Watch for wildlife along the way. Below is the view from the Fire Lookout atop Mount Washburn.

▲11 Lamar Valley (1.5 hours)

Head back north to Tower Junction and turn east for some of the
park's best wildlife viewing as you wind along the Lamar River.
Formed by receding glaciers at the end of the last ice age, the broad,
boulder-dotted grassland of the Lamar Valley
is home to a large and diverse population of
mammals, including grizzly bears, wolves, and
bison. The best times for wildlife viewing are
early morning or early evening.

Lower Lamar Valley

Drive over the Yellowstone River Bridge, just
above Tower Fall, and enjoy a snack or short hike
at the picnic area. After crossing the Lamar River,
turn north on Slough Creek Campground Road.
Stretch your legs on one of the two trails that are
accessible from the road. Bring binoculars for
some great birding.

Upper Lamar Valley

As you continue east, watch for the log buildings of Buffalo Ranch on the north side of the road. During the first half of the 1900s, the ranch raised bison to bolster the diminishing park population. Today the buildings are used by the National Park Service for residential curriculum-based education programs, and by the Yellowstone Association Institute for educational programs.

Look for bison and wolves as you continue toward the confluence of the Lamar River and Soda Butte Creek.

Pull off the road at Soda Butte to view the travertine cone of this inactive hot spring. Then stop at Trout Lake for a 1-mile, round-trip hike through a Douglas-fir forest to spot some of the resident songbirds and waterfowl. Continue following the road as it ambles along Soda Butte Creek and take in the views of the sprawling valley. Stop at the Barronette Peak Overlook for a look at Yellowstone's geological past: the limestone layers at the base of the mountain reflect a time when this area was covered by an ancient sea; the volcanic layers above reveal clues about numerous eruptions and lava flows over millions of years.

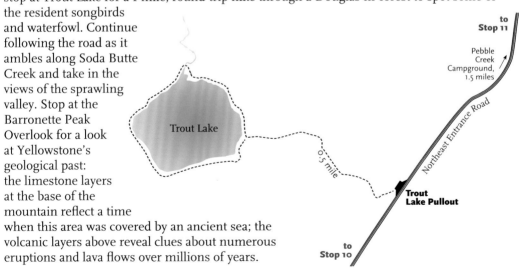

■12 Silver Gate & Cooke City

Are you a history buff? Continue on to Silver Gate and Cooke City to learn about the mining, railroad, and tourism history of the area.

Yellowstone National Park is at the heart of the Greater Yellowstone Ecosystem, a patchwork quilt of open spaces that includes two national parks, six national forests, and a number of private ranches, farmland, and rural communities. While jurisdictional boundaries exist on our maps, they are invisible to the wildlife that lives in and around the park.

Large predators, including wolves and grizzly bears, are an important part of a healthy ecosystem. This dynamic was not well understood in the early days of the park though, and wolves were hunted to extirpation. A reintroduction effort that started in 1995 has returned healthy populations of this key species to Yellowstone.

Bison are another key species that require the large swaths of open land in and around Yellowstone National Park. These large, prehistoric mammals migrate seasonally to the best forage, mating, and birthing grounds, which sometimes are neighboring ranch and farmlands. When bison leave the park, there is potential for them to trample crops or infect cows with brucellosis, a nonnative disease that was originally transmitted to bison by cattle.

A number of ecological processes create a healthy ecosystem. These include natural patterns of precipitation and fire, as well as the interactions between species, from microbes to megafauna. Park managers work closely with local and state agencies and organizations to maintain a healthy ecosystem while addressing the challenges posed by the controversies over species such as wolves and bison.

Bison Facts

* Largest land mammal North America

* Males can weigh as much as 1 ton

* Can run up to 40 miles per hour

Wildlife Day

Mammoth to Lamar Valley

Spend a day on Yellowstone's Northern Range, the Serengeti of North America.

The Northern Range spreads about 600 square miles along the northern boundary of the park and into Montana. Glaciers sculpted the wide valleys where the Lamar and Yellowstone rivers now flow, creating prime habitat and open range for many animals throughout the year.

Start early for the best chance of seeing animals that are most active at dawn. As you drive east toward Tower Junction and the Lamar Valley, watch for charismatic megafauna such as wolves, bears, bison, and elk. Look carefully for smaller fauna as well: river otters, badgers, beavers, muskrats, ground squirrels, and a variety of birds call Yellowstone home.

After a picnic lunch, stretch your legs on an afternoon hike to a beautiful, wildlife-rich mountain lake, or embark on a drive to Yellowstone's high country in search of bears, pika, and bighorn sheep.

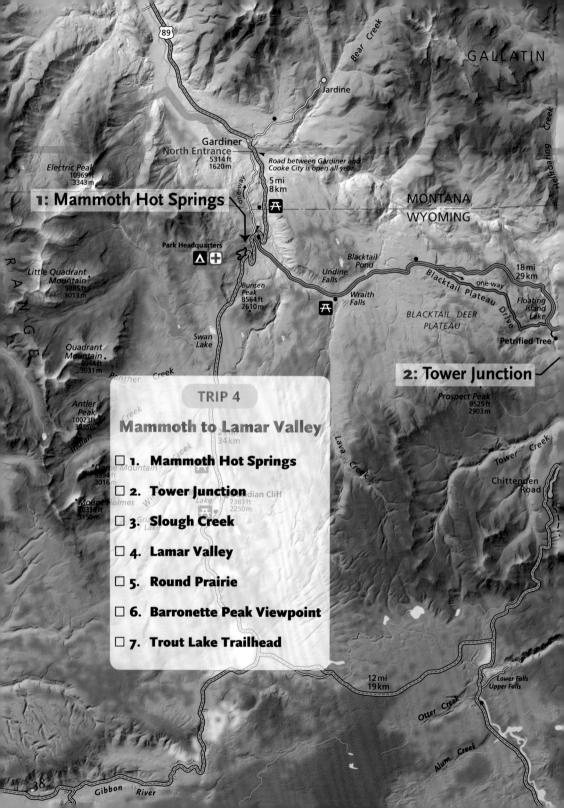

89

Bear Creek

GALLATIN

Jardine

Gardiner
North Entrance
5314 ft
1620 m

Road between Gardiner and
Cooke City is open all year

5 mi
8 km

Electric Peak
10969 ft
3343 m

1: Mammoth Hot Springs

MONTANA
WYOMING

Park Headquarters

Little Quadrant
Mountain
9885 ft
3013 m

Blacktail
Pond

Undine
Falls

18 mi
29 km

one-way

Blacktail Plateau Drive

Floating
Island
Lake

Bunsen
Peak
8564 ft
2610 m

Wraith
Falls

BLACKTAIL DEER
PLATEAU

Quadrant
Mountain
9944 ft
3031 m

Petrified Tree

Swan
Lake

Antler
Peak
10023 ft
3055 m

Panther Creek

Swan
Lake

2: Tower Junction

Prospect Peak
9525 ft
2903 m

Tower Creek

Chittenden
Road

TRIP 4

Mammoth to Lamar Valley

Dome Mountain
9894 ft
3016 m

Mount Holmes
10336 ft
3150 m

Indian Cliff
7383 ft
2250 m

Lava Creek

☐ 1. **Mammoth Hot Springs**

☐ 2. **Tower Junction**

☐ 3. **Slough Creek**

☐ 4. **Lamar Valley**

☐ 5. **Round Prairie**

☐ 6. **Barronette Peak Viewpoint**

☐ 7. **Trout Lake Trailhead**

12 mi
19 km

Lower Falls
Upper Falls

Otter Creek

Alum Creek

38

Gibbon River

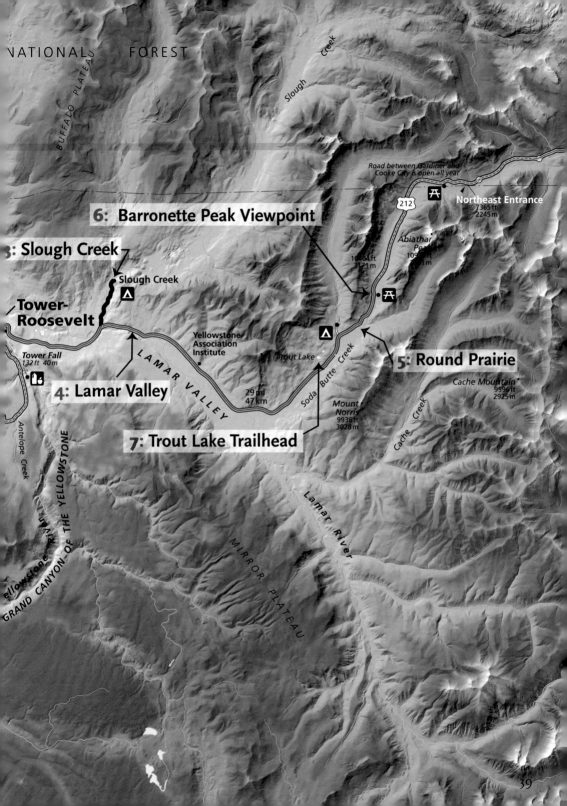

NATIONAL FOREST

BUFFALO PLATEAU

Slough Creek

Road between Gardiner and
Cooke City is open all year

212

Northeast Entrance
7365 ft
2245 m

6: Barronette Peak Viewpoint

Abiathar
Peak
10,928 ft
3331 m

10,404 ft
3171 m

3: Slough Creek

Slough Creek

**Tower-
Roosevelt**

Tower Fall
132 ft 40 m

Yellowstone
Association
Institute

5: Round Prairie

Trout Lake

4: Lamar Valley

LAMAR VALLEY

29 mi
47 km

Soda Butte Creek

Cache Mountain
9596 ft
2925 m

Cache Creek

7: Trout Lake Trailhead

Mount
Norris
9936 ft
3028 m

Antelope Creek

GRAND CANYON OF THE YELLOWSTONE

Yellowstone River

MIRROR PLATEAU

Lamar River

▶1 Mammoth Hot Springs

Begin at Mammoth Hot Springs just before daybreak. For the best wildlife viewing opportunities, plan to leave Mammoth no later than 6 a.m. during summer (June, July, and August) or by 7 a.m. the rest of the year.

■2 Tower Junction

Drive the road from Mammoth Hot Springs to Tower Junction (45 minutes, not including stops), stopping at pullouts to search for wildlife and enjoy the sunrise along the way. Look for elk and bison as you leave Mammoth; coyotes on the Blacktail Deer Plateau; waterfowl, beavers, muskrats, and blackbirds at Blacktail Pond and Floating Island Lake; and moose near Elk Creek.

At Tower Junction (restrooms available), search for bison. Turn left onto the Northeast Entrance Road.

■3 Slough Creek

On the road from Tower Junction to Slough Creek, search for pronghorn, bison, wolves, and grizzly and black bears.

Drive the unpaved Slough Creek Road (2½ miles each way; 30 minutes round-trip not including stops) to search for grizzly bears, wolves, bison, otters, muskrats, beavers, coyotes, warblers, bald and golden eagles, and waterfowl.

Things to Bring

- Binoculars and a spotting scope. Both can be rented in Gardiner, MT, five miles north of Mammoth Hot Springs.
- Field guides to mammals and birds
- Picnic lunch

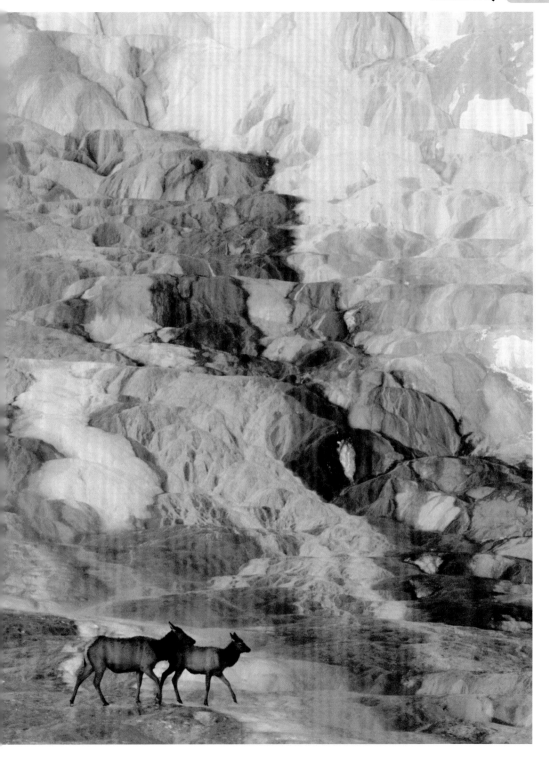

◀4 **Lamar Valley**
Return to the main road and continue east to Lamar Valley (10 minutes, not including stops), searching for osprey and red fox in Lamar Canyon. In Lamar Valley, stop often at pullouts to search for wolves, grizzly and black bears, bison, pronghorn, coyotes, elk, and raptors such as bald and golden eagles, ospreys, and prairie falcons.

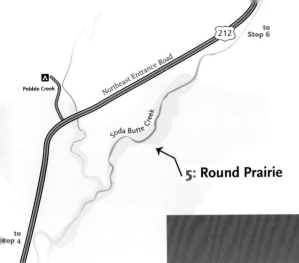

Pebble Creek

212
to
Stop 6

Northeast Entrance Road

Soda Butte Creek

5: Round Prairie

to
top 4

◀5 Round Prairie

Continue from the east end of Lamar Valley to the unsigned area called Round Prairie, just past the Pebble Creek turnoff. Scan the willows for moose, search the forest edges for coyotes, foxes, wolves, and bears, and scour the slopes of the Absaroka Mountains for other wildlife.

▶6 Barronette Peak Viewpoint

Drive east 10 minutes (not including stops) to the Barronette Peak Viewpoint. Enjoy your picnic lunch while looking for mountain goats and admiring the countless waterfalls on the mountainside, or drive to Warm Creek Picnic Area (good moose habitat) or Soda Butte Picnic Area (look for black bears and coyotes) for lunch (toilets available at both sites). Rich forests in this part of the park provide habitat for Clark's nutcrackers, gray jays, pine martens, and red squirrels.

Photos by Jim Peaco, NPS

You are most likely to encounter **bears** at park roadsides. If you see a bear while driving, do not stop and do not block any portion of the road. Regardless of what other people do, keep moving to the next paved pullout and park safely. If the bear is within 100 yards, watch and take photographs from inside your car.

■7 Trout Lake Trailhead

For an afternoon hike, drive west to the Trout Lake Trailhead. A ½-mile dirt path climbs to Trout Lake, a placid lake in the shadow of the Absaroka Mountains. As you follow the path around the lake, watch for river otters, cutthroat trout, waterfowl, and badgers. To extend your hike, follow the path from the inlet of Trout Lake another half mile to Buck Lake. Return to the trailhead by the same route.

To return to Mammoth Hot Springs, retrace your driving route (1.5 hours, not including stops). See the map on pages 38 and 39.

Alternative Trip: Dunraven Pass

Instead of hiking after lunch, return to Tower Junction, turn left onto the Tower to Canyon Road, and drive to Dunraven Pass (30 minutes each way, not including stops). The alpine meadows of the Washburn Range, visible along this stretch of road, are home to black and grizzly bears, especially in late summer (August) when these bears travel to higher elevations in search of whitebark pine nuts. The slopes of Mount Washburn also host bighorn sheep and pika.

Yellowstone's Northern Range is home to one of the largest and most diverse populations of large mammals on Earth. But what is the Northern Range?

Yellowstone's Northern Range is a grassland and sagebrush habitat surrounding the Yellowstone River and its tributaries in the northern portion of the park. The Northern Range supports dense populations of large mammals year-round. Lower elevations and drier winters make the Northern Range especially valuable as winter habitat for many of the park's ungulates (large hoofed mammals)—and also for their predators.

Where are all the bears? What about the wolves? Finding wildlife in the wide-open spaces of northern Yellowstone can be a challenge. To aid your search and make your wildlife-watching day more successful, remember that all animals need the same things we do: food and a good home. What do certain animals eat? If you are searching for bison, look for rich grasslands with plenty of forage. Since bison cool themselves by evaporating water from their lungs, they also need plenty of water to drink on hot summer days. Bears are omnivores, and their food preferences change with the seasons. In spring, grizzlies hunt elk calves, and both grizzly and black bears munch on green grass, ants, and spring wildflowers. Downed logs house insects that are a delicacy to bears.

Black bear

rump is higher than shoulders

no shoulder hump

straight face profile

Later in the summer, bears travel to high elevations in search of whitebark pine nuts. They scavenge throughout the spring, summer, and fall. In contrast, wolves are strictly carnivores. About 80-90% of a wolf's diet here in Yellowstone is elk, so if you are searching for wolves, search also for elk. Do the elk look nervous? Are there ravens or eagles around that may be scavenging on a wolf kill? Do you hear a coyote barking an alarm at the approach of a wolf? As you drive through Yellowstone's Northern Range, stop often, get out of your vehicle, and look and listen carefully for wildlife and their clues.

Grizzly bear

dished
face profile

short
round ears

distinct shoulder hump

Birding Day
Madison River to Mammoth

Water is the key to finding birds in Yellowstone.
Areas with aspens, cottonwoods, and shrubby willows attract a
wide variety of songbirds for nesting and foraging in summer.
Streams, rivers, lakes, and ponds are all good for birds,
especially those with vegetation at the edges that provides
protective cover for birds and their nests. Areas with high plant
diversity have a greater variety and abundance of birds.

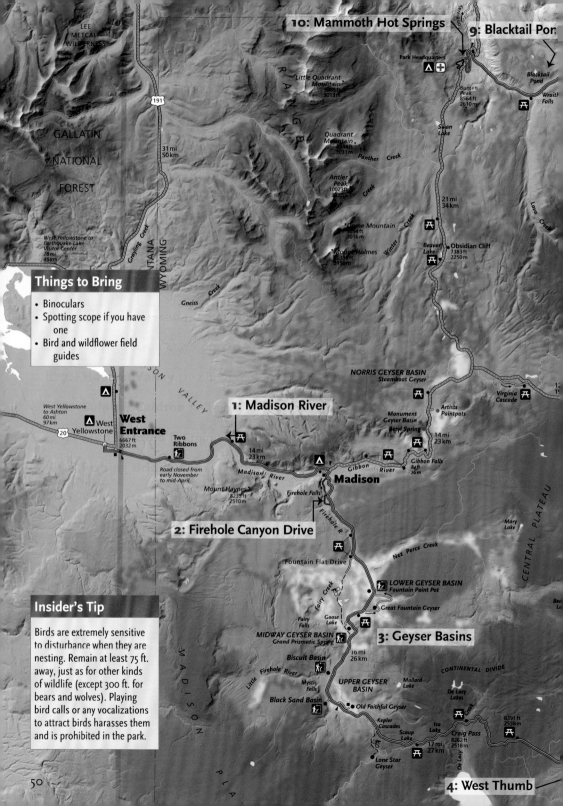

LEE METCALF WILDERNESS

Little Quadrant Mountain 9885 ft 3013 m

Park Headquarters

Blacktail Pond

Bunsen Peak 8564 ft 2610 m

Wraith Falls

191

GALLATIN

NATIONAL

FOREST

31 mi 50 km

Quadrant Mountain 9944 ft 3031 m

Panther Creek

Swan Lake

Antler Peak 10023 ft 3055 m

Indian Creek

21 mi 34 km

Lava Creek

West Yellowstone to Earthquake Lake Visitor Center 28 mi 45 km

Grayling Creek

MONTANA WYOMING

Dome Mountain 9894 ft 3016 m

Winter Creek

Mount Holmes 10336 ft 3150 m

Beaver Lake

Obsidian Cliff 7383 ft 2250 m

Gneiss Creek

Things to Bring

- Binoculars
- Spotting scope if you have one
- Bird and wildflower field guides

NORRIS GEYSER BASIN
Steamboat Geyser

Artists Paintpots

Virginia Cascade

1: Madison River

West Yellowstone to Ashton 60 mi 97 km

20

West Yellowstone

West Entrance 6667 ft 2032 m

Two Ribbons

14 mi 23 km

Monument Geyser Basin

Beryl Spring

14 mi 23 km

Gibbon River

Gibbon Falls 84 ft 26 m

Road closed from early November to mid-April

Madison River

Madison

Mount Haynes 8235 ft 2510 m

Firehole Falls

2: Firehole Canyon Drive

Firehole R.

Nez Perce Creek

Mary Lake

CENTRAL PLATEAU

Fountain Flat Drive

Insider's Tip

Birds are extremely sensitive to disturbance when they are nesting. Remain at least 75 ft. away, just as for other kinds of wildlife (except 300 ft. for bears and wolves). Playing bird calls or any vocalizations to attract birds harasses them and is prohibited in the park.

Fairy Creek

LOWER GEYSER BASIN
Fountain Paint Pot

Great Fountain Geyser

Fairy Falls

Goose Lake

MIDWAY GEYSER BASIN
Grand Prismatic Spring

3: Geyser Basins

16 mi 26 km

Biscuit Basin

CONTINENTAL DIVIDE

MADISON

Little Firehole River

Mystic Falls

Black Sand Basin

UPPER GEYSER BASIN

Mallard Lake

De Lacy Lakes

8391 ft 2558 m

Old Faithful Geyser

Kepler Cascades

Scaup Lake

Isa Lake

Craig Pass 8262 ft 2518 m

17 mi 27 km

De Lacy Creek

Lone Star Geyser

MADISON PLA

50

4: West Thumb

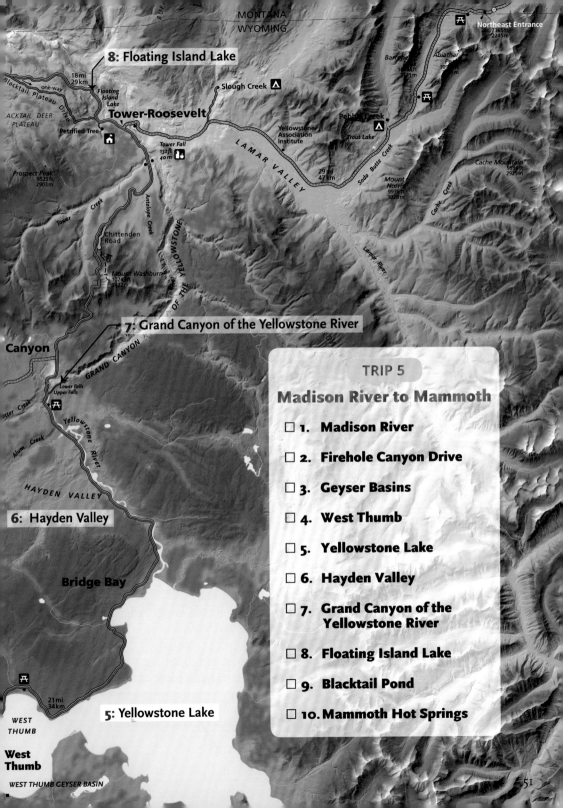

MONTANA
WYOMING

Northeast Entrance
7365 ft
2245 m

8: Floating Island Lake

18 mi
29 km

one-way

Blacktail Plateau Drive

Floating
Island
Lake

Slough Creek

ACKTAIL DEER
PLATEAU

Barnone
Peak
10928 ft

Abiathar
Pk
1093 m

Tower-Roosevelt

Petrified Tree

Pebble Creek

Yellowstone
Association
Institute

Trout Lake

Tower Fall
132 ft
40 m

Prospect Peak
9525 ft
2903 m

LAMAR VALLEY

Cache Mountain
9966 ft
2925 m

Tower Creek

Antelope Creek

Chittenden
Road

29 mi
47 km

Soda Butte Creek

Mount
Norris
9936 ft
3028 m

Cache Creek

Mount Washburn
10245 ft
3122 m

Lamar River

GRAND CANYON OF THE YELLOWSTONE

7: Grand Canyon of the Yellowstone River

Canyon

GRAND CANYON

Lower Falls
Upper Falls

tter Creek

Yellowstone River

Alum Creek

HAYDEN VALLEY

6: Hayden Valley

Bridge Bay

21 mi
34 km

5: Yellowstone Lake

WEST
THUMB

West Thumb

WEST THUMB GEYSER BASIN

51

Barrow's Goldeneye *Bucephala islandica*

Sandhill Crane *Grus canadensis*

Clark's Nutcracker *Nucifraga columbiana*

Canada Goose *Branta canadensis*

Common Merganser *Mergus merganser*

Photos by Henry Hodsworth

■1 Madison River

Drive east along the Madison River toward Madison Junction. Stop at pullouts along the way to view waterfowl, great blue herons, sandhill cranes, spotted sandpipers, and occasionally other shorebirds. Keep an eye out for bald eagles and ospreys, both of which nest near the river. Listen for the trill melodies of songbirds in June and early July.

■2 Firehole Canyon Drive

Turn south at Madison Junction onto the Grand Loop Road and take the first right onto Firehole Canyon Drive. Stop at turnouts along this side road to look for American dippers and ospreys.

American Dipper
Cinclus mexicanus

■3 Geyser Basins

Stop at each of the geyser basins (Lower Geyser, Midway Geyser, Upper Geyser, Biscuit, and Black Sand) to stretch your legs, explore the area, and watch for mountain bluebirds and a variety of sparrows. For easier parking and to avoid crowds, visit these areas early in the day or in the late afternoon or early evening. Take a walk around Old Faithful and look for ospreys hunting for fish in the Firehole River.

■4 West Thumb

Drive east from Old Faithful toward Yellowstone Lake. Turn north at West Thumb to follow the shoreline of the lake. Stop along the way to watch for waterfowl and other water birds, such as common loons and western grebes. September and October are good months to see these migratory birds in Yellowstone.

■5 Yellowstone Lake

Continue north along the western edge of Yellowstone Lake toward Fishing Bridge.

For an optional side trip, drive east from Fishing Bridge along the northeast perimeter of the lake and stop at pullouts and trailheads for more opportunities to see migratory and resident waterfowl and water birds. There are many lakes and ponds along the East Entrance road that offer exceptional birding opportunities.

Spotted Sandpiper *Actitis macularia*

Osprey *Pandion haliaetus*

Mountain Bluebird *Sialia currucoides*

Common Loon *Gavia immer*

Western Grebe *Aechmophorus occidentalis*

■6 Hayden Valley

Continue north from Fishing Bridge into Hayden Valley. This stretch of the road follows the course of the Yellowstone River through the valley, which is excellent habitat for wildlife, from bison to birds. Hayden Valley provides nest sites for vesper, savannah, and white-crowned sparrows, to few, in the grass and sagebrush meadow ... ie Yellowstone River. Waterfowl congreg ... ow-moving waters. Watch for Canada g ... ducks, including gadwalls, America ... and mallards; and diving ducks, su ... goldeneyes and common mergans ... adjacent to the river look for Americaii a ... spotted sandpipers. Scan the skies for Sw ... hawks, red-tailed hawks, and bald eagles, a : ... raptor species that nest in the valley. Septen: ... October are good months for spotting raptors.

■7 Grand Canyon of the Yellowstone River

Continue north to Canyon Village. At Canyon Junction, drive the North and South Rim drives along the Grand Canyon of the Yellowstone. While enjoying views of the Lower and Upper Falls (from the South Rim), keep an eye out for swooping and diving violet-green swallows, white-throated swifts, and peregrine and prairie falcons. Ospreys

Great Blue Heron
Ardea herodias

Peregrine Falcon
Falco peregrinus

Cliff swallow *Petrochelidon pyrrhonota*

Yellow-headed blackbird
Xanthocephalus xanthocephalus

Mallard *Anas platyrhynchos*

nest on pillars in the canyon, so you can use binoculars to watch their nesting behaviors and their fuzzy youngsters during the summer months. Clark's nutcrackers and common ravens cruise over the canyon and call from the whitebark pines that rim the canyon walls.

■8 Floating Island Lake

Continue north along the Grand Loop Road toward Tower Junction. Head west at the junction and stop at Floating Island Lake. The lake attracts a number of migratory birds, as well as many year-round residents. In summer, watch for waterfowl, sandhill cranes, and yellow-headed blackbirds.

Insider's Tip

Complete raptor observation and rare bird forms to document your sightings. Both forms are available at visitor centers and on the park website.

For an optional side trip and great hike, drive east from Tower Junction to Slough Creek. The Slough Creek Trail hosts a variety of songbirds and woodpeckers from June through September. Where the trail is close to the creek, look for waterfowl and sandhill cranes. Colorful wildflowers line the trail in June, July, and early August. Enjoy spectacular views of Cutoff Mountain and other peaks in the Absaroka Range.

■9 Blacktail Pond

Continue driving west toward Mammoth Hot Springs

and stop at Blacktail Pond for a chance to view
many bird species, along with other resident
wildlife. During summer, and the spring and
fall migration periods, watch for a variety of
warblers and sparrows. Mallards, Barrow's
goldeneyes, Townsend's solitaires, common
ravens, and mountain chickadees call this
riparian area home year-round.

▶10 Mammoth Hot Springs

At Mammoth Hot Springs, end your day with a
short trek at Beaver Ponds. Access the trailhead
from Clematis Gulch between Liberty Cap and
the stone house. Beaver Ponds Trail provides
habitat for many kinds of songbirds from May
through August, along with great wildflower
displays from May through July. Waterfowl,
pied-billed grebes, sora, American coots,
yellow-headed blackbirds, and red-winged
blackbirds are some of the birds nesting in the
marshy areas surrounding the ponds.

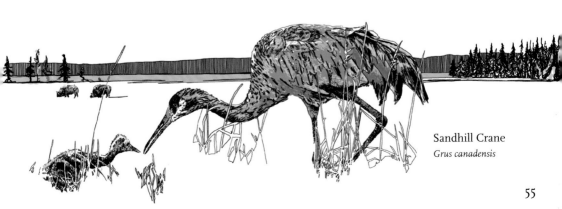

Sandhill Crane
Grus canadensis

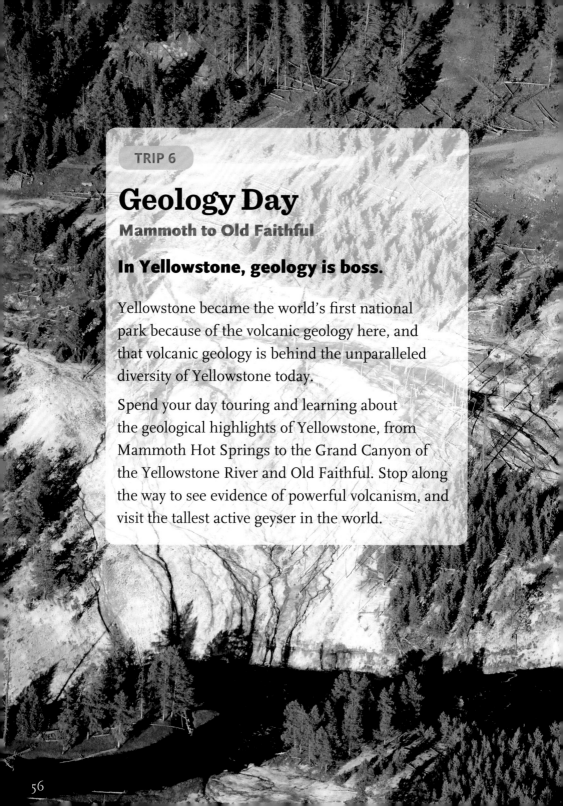

Geology Day
Mammoth to Old Faithful

In Yellowstone, geology is boss.

Yellowstone became the world's first national park because of the volcanic geology here, and that volcanic geology is behind the unparalleled diversity of Yellowstone today.

Spend your day touring and learning about the geological highlights of Yellowstone, from Mammoth Hot Springs to the Grand Canyon of the Yellowstone River and Old Faithful. Stop along the way to see evidence of powerful volcanism, and visit the tallest active geyser in the world.

1: Mammoth Hot Springs

5: Hellroaring Overlook

2: Mt. Everts

3: Undine Falls

4: Wraith Falls

6: Petrified Tree

8: Mt. Washburr

11: Norris Geyser Basin

12: Gibbon Falls and Gibbon River

OPTIONAL SIDE TRIP: Hayden Valley

13: Firehole Canyon Drive

15: Midway Geyser Basin

14: Fountain Paint Pot

16: Old Faithful

Jardine

89

Gardiner
North Entrance
5314 ft
1620 m

Electric Peak
10969 ft
3343 m

Park Headquarters

Little Quadrant
Mountain
9885 ft
3013 m

Bunsen
Peak
8564 ft
2610 m

Undine
Falls

Blacktail
Pond

Blacktail Plateau Drive

one-way

BLACKTAIL DEER
PLATEAU

Wraith
Falls

Petrified

191

Quadrant
Mountain
9931 m

Swan
Lake

BLACKTAIL DEER
PLATEAU

31 mi
50 km

Antler
Peak
10023 ft
3055 m

Panther Creek

Lava Creek

21 mi
34 km

MONTANA
WYOMING

Dome Mountain
9884 ft
3016 m

Winter Creek

Mount Holmes
10336 ft
3150 m

Beaver
Lake

Obsidian Cliff
7383 ft
2250 m

Grizzly
Lake

Gneiss Creek

MADISON
VALLEY

NORRIS GEYSER BASIN
Steamboat Geyser

Canyon

12 mi
19 km

Virginia
Cascade

Lower Fa
Upper Falls

Artists
Paintpots

Otter Creek

Yello

**West
Entrance**
6667 ft
2032 m

Two
Ribbons

14 mi
23 km

14 mi
23 km

Gibbon Falls
84 ft
26 m

Alum Creek

HAYDEN

Madison

Gibbon River

HAYDEN VALLEY

Road closed from
early November
to mid-April

Madison River

Firehole Falls

Mount Haynes
8235 ft
2510 m

CENTRAL PLATEAU

Firehole R.

Nez Perce Creek

Beach
Lake

Fountain Flat Drive

Fairy Creek

LOWER GEYSER BASIN
Fountain Paint Pot

Goose
Lake

CONTINENTAL DIVIDE

MADISON

MIDWAY GEYSER BASIN
Grand Prismatic Spring

16 mi
26 km

De Lacy
Lakes

Biscuit Basin

UPPER GEYSER BASIN

Mallard
Lake

Little Firehole River

Mystic Falls

8391 ft
2558 m

21 mi
34 km

Black Sand Basin

Old Faithful Geyser

Kepler
Cascades

Isa
Lake

Craig Pass
8262 ft
2518 m

**WEST
THUMB**

Scaup
Lake

17 mi
27 km

De Lacy Creek

Lone Star
Geyser

58

LEE
METCALF
WILDERNESS

RANGE

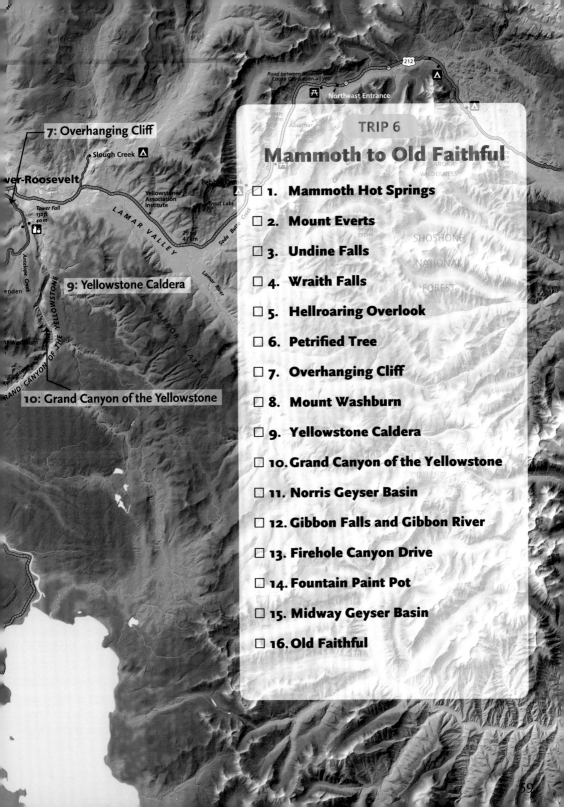

7: Overhanging Cliff

9: Yellowstone Caldera

10: Grand Canyon of the Yellowstone

▲1 Mammoth Hot Springs

Start the day watching some of the mesmerizing hydrothermal activity and exploring geological processes happening right before your eyes at Mammoth Hot Springs. Limestone, a sedimentary rock composed of calcium carbonate that was deposited on the bed of an ancient inland sea, underlies this area. Hot water dissolves the limestone and becomes saturated with calcium carbonate. When the water nears the surface, pressure and temperature decrease, allowing carbon dioxide gas to escape from the solution (like opening a can of soda). The resulting deposits of calcium carbonate that form in and near the hot springs are called travertine, the white rock that dominates the landscape here at Mammoth.

Fresh travertine is bright white, but it turns gray as it weathers. Because travertine is a soft rock, it both breaks down and builds up rapidly. Some studies indicate that travertine builds up at an average rate of 8 inches per year. For this reason, change is the only constant at Mammoth. Terraces that were active one year might be dry the next, and new areas become active and build terraces at this geologically stunning rate.

You may also notice areas that appear orange or yellow in color. These colors are thermophiles, heat-loving organisms such as bacteria and algae that thrive in the warm waters of hot springs throughout the park.

While at Mammoth, look for Liberty Cap, a 37-foot-tall cone formed by an extinct hot spring and Palette Spring, an active and colorful hot spring.

◀1 **Palette Spring**

■2 Mount Everts

As you drive east from Mammoth to Tower Junction, notice the ridge dominating the view to the north. Mount Everts demonstrates much of the geologic history of the region.

The bulk of Everts is sedimentary rock that was deposited in the Cretaceous Interior Seaway about 100 million years ago. The bottom third of Everts is the Telegraph Creek Formation, sandstone and shale that formed from mud deposited in about 100 feet of water far off shore. As the level of the Seaway began to drop, the shoreline moved eastward, and depositions in the Yellowstone area changed. Above the Telegraph Creek Formation, the Eagle Formation (the middle third of Everts) is sandstone deposited in much shallower water near the shoreline. After the shoreline retreated to the east of the Yellowstone Region, this area was part of a swampy coastal plain where rivers meandered eastward toward the remnants of the Seaway. As they did so, these rivers deposited sediment that became the shale of the Everts Formation, now the top third of Mount Everts. Because the Telegraph Creek, Eagle, and Everts Formations were deposited sequentially as the shoreline of the sea retreated, the formations together are called a regressive sedimentary sequence.

**Huckleberry Ridge Caldera
(formed 2.1 million years ago)**

The very top of Mount Everts is capped by a band of cliffs formed from volcanic rock of a much more recent origin. The Huckleberry Ridge Tuff is volcanic ash that blanketed this area following the first major eruption in this region of the Yellowstone Supervolcano about 2.1 million years ago. If you look closely at the Huckleberry Ridge Tuff with binoculars, you can see the reddish color of baked shale beneath the ash; the ash was so hot when it fell that it baked the shale of the Everts Formation to a depth of more than 30 feet.

■3 Undine Falls

As you continue east, watch for a variety of other volcanic deposits, including basalts, ashes, and rhyolites. Stop at Undine Falls to see where Lava Creek flows over a 700,000-year-old basalt lava flow, which rests on top of weaker shale. Weaker rock beneath harder volcanic rock results in uneven erosion, creating the falls.

**Island Park Caldera
(formed 1.3 million years ago
and created Mesa Falls Tuff)**

■4 Wraith Falls

As you continue toward Wraith Falls, watch for places where Lava Creek Tuff, from the last major volcanic eruption 640,000 years ago, is exposed.

■5 Hellroaring Overlook

Stop at this overlook, about 12 miles east of Mammoth, for an excellent view of the Yellowstone River and Hellroaring Creek valleys. The gray-pink peaks to the north, including cone-shaped Hellroaring Mountain, are Precambrian granite and gneiss. These ancient rocks (more than 2 billion years old) are the southernmost outcrop of the Beartooth Uplift.

**Lava Creek Caldera
(formed 64 million years ago)**

■6 Petrified Tree

About 16½ miles east of Mammoth, stop to see an ancient redwood that was turned to stone. About 50 million years ago, this area was buried beneath silica-rich ash and debris from the Absaroka Volcanics. As water filtered down through this volcanic debris, it dissolved silica. When the water came into contact with buried organic material such as this redwood, silica was deposited and coated the organic material, preserving the tree in stone.

■7 Overhanging Cliff

As you travel southeast from Tower Junction to Canyon Village, watch for the Overhanging Cliff between Calcite Springs Overlook and Tower Fall.

The Overhanging Cliff is 2.2 million-year-old Junction Butte Basalt, one of the oldest lava flows in this region from the Yellowstone Hotspot. The distinct columnar jointing formed as the lava cooled and solidified.

▼8 Mount Washburn

Continue south and the road climbs toward Mount Washburn and Dunraven Pass. Mount Washburn is the remnant of a 50 million-year-old volcano of the Absaroka Volcanics. Compared to the rhyolites of the present-day Yellowstone volcanism, the andesites of the Absaroka Volcanics weather to more nutrient-rich soils that also hold more moisture than do rhyolitic soils. At the elevations on the flanks of Mount Washburn (8,000 feet and higher), these andesitic soils support whitebark pine trees. In late summer, look for grizzly and black bears feeding on the nuts of the whitebark pines as the bears devour 20,000 calories per day in preparation for hibernation.

◄9 Yellowstone Caldera

As you continue south from Dunraven Pass, you see the Yellowstone Caldera before you. At about 640,000 years old, this is the youngest and second largest of three calderas in and near the park. When the supervolcano erupted 640,000 years ago, an area of land about 30 miles by 45 miles collapsed to fill the void left by the empty magma chamber below. This steep-sided and flat-bottomed caldera

Silky phacelia in bloom along Chittenden Road below Mount Washburn.

Photo by Diane Renkin

has since been masked by erosion and subsequent lava flows, and as such is now largely invisible. Where portions of the caldera are visible, its sheer size makes it difficult to comprehend. On a clear day, stop at the Washburn Hot Springs Overlook and look for the Red Mountains about 35 miles to the south. Most geologists agree that prior to the last eruption of the Yellowstone Supervolcano, the Red Mountains and the Washburn Range (where you now stand) were connected by a range of mountains that completely disappeared when they collapsed into the caldera 640,000 years ago.

■10 Grand Canyon of the Yellowstone

Pick up a trail map and brochure at the Visitor Center or at one of the viewpoints or trailheads. Walk the South Rim Trail, visit the viewpoints along North Rim Drive, and view geology exhibits at the Canyon Visitor Education Center.

About half a million years ago, following the most recent volcanic eruption, the canyon area was covered by a rhyolite lava flow. After that time, this area probably looked similar to present-day geyser basins: a river, the ancestral Yellowstone River, flowed among geysers, hot springs, mudpots, and fumaroles. As the hot water of the thermal features flowed through the hard rhyolite, heat and chemical interactions baked and weakened the rock. As the Yellowstone River flowed through this weakened rock near the end of the Pinedale Glaciation, the river cut down through the rock. Today, evidence of thermal activity persists as streaks of yellow sulphur and red iron in the colorful canyon walls, and steam rising from the canyon on cool mornings.

The Caldera

These three schematic diagrams show the idealized stages in the development of the Yellowstone Caldera 640,000 years ago.

Approximately 2 miles south of Canyon Junction, turn left to access the viewpoints for the Upper Falls and Artist Point. The Upper Falls are first, then continue straight ahead until you reach the parking area for Artist Point. As you walk from the parking area to Artist Point, keep looking left for views of the canyon and back toward the Lower Falls. Late afternoon provides dramatic lighting and colors on the canyon walls when looking toward the falls from this area. Continue on to both the upper and lower viewpoints at Artist Point.

Optional Side Trip: Hayden Valley

Photo by Jason P Ross, dreamstime

If time allows, detour south into Hayden Valley to search for wildlife before continuing to Norris. Geology largely determines where plants and animals live. During the Pinedale Glaciation, ice dams twice formed at the north end of present-day Hayden Valley, damming the ancestral Yellowstone River and turning Hayden Valley into a large glacial lake. Clays and other nutrient-rich and moisture-holding lake-bottom sediments were deposited and persist today, making Hayden Valley one of the richest habitats in the park.

▼11 Norris Geyser Basin

Stop at the trailhead to pick up a trail map and brochure to guide you through your walk at Norris. Loop trails through the Porcelain and Back basins take you close to the unique features of the area.

Norris Geyser Basin is the hottest, most dynamic geyser basin in Yellowstone, likely because it rests at the intersection of three different fault systems. Home to the largest active geyser in the world (Steamboat Geyser, which erupts up to 300 feet high), Norris also contains rare acidic geysers such as Echinus, which erupts infrequently. Acidic geysers are rare because geysers require great pressure in order to erupt, and acidic water weakens and breaks down rock, causing the rock to fail at lower pressures than geysers require.

Photo by Kwiktor, dreamstime

Echinus Geyser

In addition to Norris's world-famous geysers, this area also hosts unique thermophilic organisms such as *Zygogonium*, a green alga that is photosynthetic but also uses chemical nutrients from the hot springs. The black color of *Zygogonium* is like sunblock, protecting the algae from sun-related cell damage. When *Zygogonium* is damaged by the sun, however, it can repair that damage at the cellular level!

■12 Gibbon Falls and Gibbon River

Continue south toward Madison Junction and stop at Gibbon Falls. Take the short walkway to view the falls, where the Gibbon River plunges over the caldera rim.

As you continue southwest along the Gibbon River, notice evidence of the 1988 fires. The young lodgepole pines that are recolonizing this area grow on rhyolitic lava flows that are younger than 640,000 years. Because rhyolite is poor in nutrients, it weathers to a poor, dry soil that only lodgepole pines can tolerate.

■13 Firehole Canyon Drive

If time allows, drive the one-way Firehole Canyon Drive. This road travels along the Firehole River as the river careens between two lava flows. On your left is the Nez Perce Flow, which came from a vent near Mary Mountain, 12 miles to the east. Look closely to see breccia (broken, angular rocks) created as the top of the flow hardened while the center continued to move, causing the hardened portion to break.

On the opposite side of the river is the West Yellowstone Flow, which emanated from a vent about 15 miles from here, at the western edge of the caldera, around 110,000 years ago. The dark areas in the canyon wall are shattered volcanic glass called hyaloclastite, formed when the lava mixed rapidly with water, causing the lava to cool very quickly. The West Yellowstone Flow was stopped here by the older Nez Perce Flow, and the Firehole River has since carved its canyon in the weak rock between the two flows.

▼14 Fountain Paint Pot

Stop at the trailhead to pick up a trail map and brochure. You can see all four types of hydrothermal features on this trail: hot springs, geysers, mudpots, and fumaroles. Each feature requires the same ingredients: plumbing (cracks in the earth through which water can flow), heat, earthquakes (to keep the plumbing systems from clogging themselves), and water. The water comes from the rain and snow that falls each winter on the Yellowstone Plateau. As the snow melts each spring, water percolates down through cracks in the earth until it comes into contact with heated brine a few miles beneath the surface. Because hot water is less dense than cold water, the hot water begins to rise back toward the surface and emerges as one of the types of hydrothermal features depending on the plumbing in the area.

From Fountain Paint Pot, you can also look to the north and see the northern rim of the caldera (the most distant tree-lined ridge) and the West Yellowstone Lava Flow (the tree-covered ridge in front of the caldera rim). Here, the West Yellowstone Flow probably flowed against a glacier. Looking west from the road north or south of Fountain Paint Pot, you can see additional evidence of glaciers in the Twin Buttes, hydrothermally altered glacial kames that consist of glacial debris deposited in areas of the glacier that were melted by thermal activity beneath the glacier.

Photo by Frank Kovalchek

**Grand Prismatic Spring
and Midway Geyser
Basin**

▲15 Midway Geyser Basin

On the road south of Fountain Paint Pot, you will pass
Midway Geyser Basin, the location of Grand Prismatic
Spring, the largest hot spring in the park, and Excelsior
Geyser Crater, which expels 4,000 gallons of boiling water
per minute into the Firehole River.

◄16 Old Faithful

Stop at the Old Faithful Visitor Education
Center for the next predicted eruptions of Old
Faithful Geyser and other large geysers in the
Upper Geyser Basin and view exhibits and
films explaining thermal features. The center
has a special young scientist room aimed at
children. If time allows, pick up a trail map
brochure from the visitor center and tour the
boardwalks of the Upper Geyser Basin to see
the highest concentration of geysers in the
world.

Hydrothermal Feature: Geysers

Geysers are hot springs with constrictions in their plumbing, usually near the surface, that prevent water from circulating freely to the surface where heat would escape. The deepest circulating water can exceed the surface boiling point (199°F/93°C). Surrounding pressure also increases with depth, similar to the ocean. Increased pressure exerted by the enormous weight of the overlying water prevents the water from boiling. As the water rises, steam forms. Bubbling upward, steam expands as it nears the top of the water column. At a critical point, the confined bubbles actually lift the water above, causing the geyser to splash or overflow. This decreases pressure on the system, and violent boiling results. Tremendous amounts of steam force water out of the vent, and an eruption begins. Water is expelled faster than it can enter the geyser's plumbing system, and the heat and pressure gradually decrease. The eruption stops when the water reservoir is depleted or when the system cools.

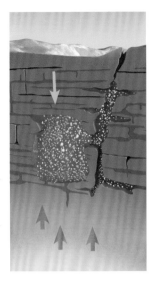

Moisture from snow and rain percolate down through porous rock layers.

Magma just miles below the surface provides heat.

Weight of water above causes pressure and heat to build below.

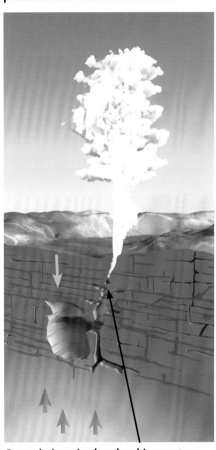

Constrictions in the plumbing system cause water and steam to explode with force.

Illustration based on information found in "The plumbing of Old Faithful Geyser revealed by hydrothermal tremor," by Jean Vandemeulebrouck, professional paper, 2013.

Things to Bring

- Wide angle lens (24 mm or wider)

- Mid-range zoom lens

- Telephoto lens (200–300 mm)

- Macro lens

- Tripod

- Cable release

- Polarizing filter

- Bear spray

- Bug repellent

- Sunscreen

- Water

- Snacks

- Binoculars

NOTE: Be sure to check the contents of your photo bag before you arrive. Very limited photographic supplies are available in Yellowstone, and the nearest camera store is 80 miles away.

TRIP 7

Photography Day

Mammoth to Swan Lake Flats

Yellowstone is one of the world's premier photographic destinations.

There are photo opportunities in every direction and at all times of day in Yellowstone National Park. Scenery, wildlife, geology, the unique patterns and colors of the thermal areas, and a diverse offering of botanicals offer an unparalleled photographic experience at any time of year.

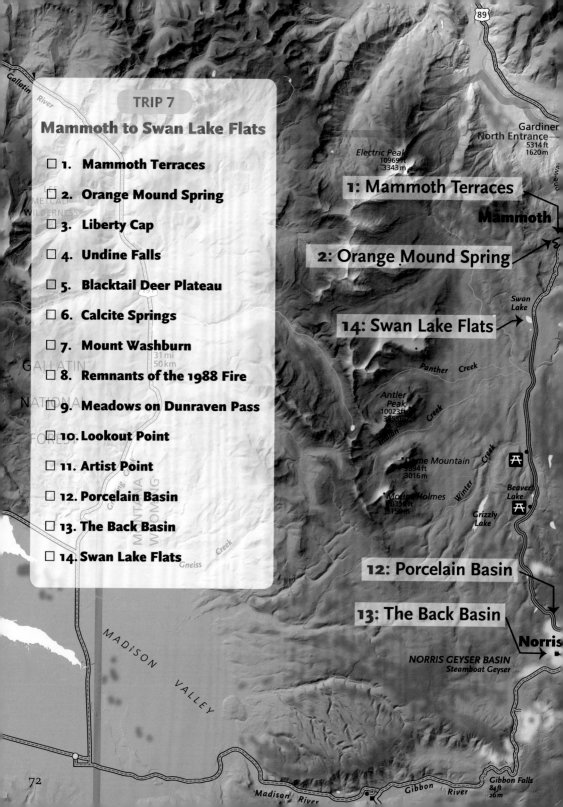

1: Mammoth Terraces

Mammoth

2: Orange Mound Spring

14: Swan Lake Flats

12: Porcelain Basin

13: The Back Basin

Norris

NORRIS GEYSER BASIN
Steamboat Geyser

Gardiner
North Entrance
5314 ft
1620 m

Electric Peak
10969 ft
3343 m

Swan
Lake

Panther   Creek

Antler
Peak
10023 ft
3455 m

Dome Mountain
9894 ft
3016 m

Mount Holmes
10336 ft
3150 m

Grizzly
Lake

Beaver
Lake

Winter   Creek

GALLATIN

NATIONAL

FOREST

LEE
METCALF
WILDERNESS

Gallatin   River

31 mi
50 km

MONTANA
WYOMING

Gneiss   Creek

MADISON   VALLEY

Madison   River

Gibbon   River

Gibbon Falls
84 ft
26 m

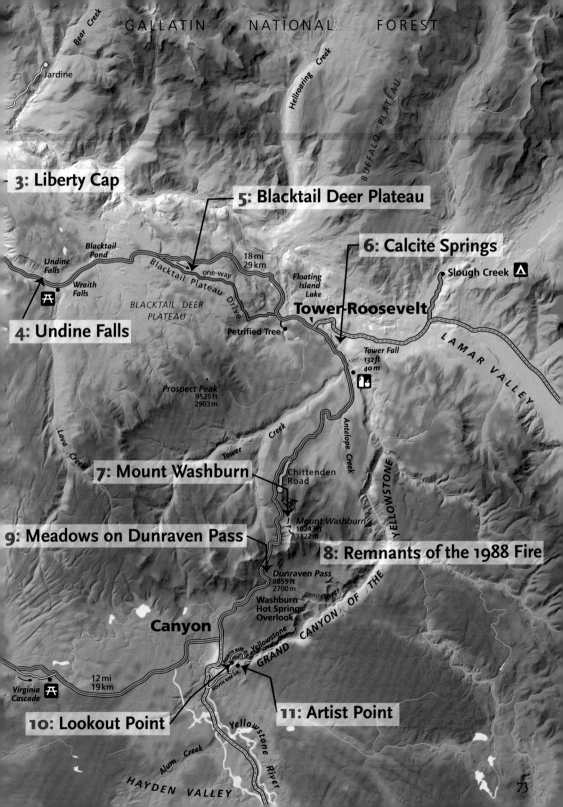

GALLATIN NATIONAL FOREST

Bear Creek

Jardine

Hellroaring Creek

BUFFALO PLATEAU

3: Liberty Cap

5: Blacktail Deer Plateau

6: Calcite Springs

Blacktail Pond

Undine Falls

Blacktail Plateau Drive

one-way

18 mi
29 km

Floating Island Lake

Slough Creek

Wraith Falls

BLACKTAIL DEER PLATEAU

Tower-Roosevelt

LAMAR VALLEY

4: Undine Falls

Petrified Tree

Tower Fall
132 ft
40 m

Prospect Peak
9525 ft
2903 m

Lava Creek

Tower Creek

Antelope Creek

7: Mount Washburn

Chittenden Road

Mount Washburn
10243 ft
3122 m

YELLOWSTONE

9: Meadows on Dunraven Pass

8: Remnants of the 1988 Fire

Dunraven Pass
8859 ft
2700 m

Washburn Hot Springs Overlook

Yellowstone River

GRAND CANYON OF THE

Canyon

NORTH RIM DR

Yellowstone

12 mi
19 km

SOUTH RIM DR.

Virginia Cascade

11: Artist Point

10: Lookout Point

Alum Creek

Yellowstone River

HAYDEN VALLEY

73

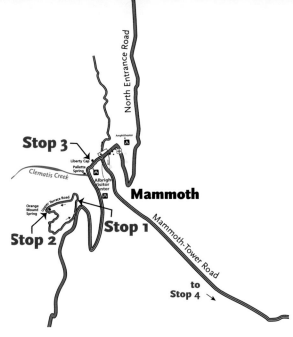

◀1 Mammoth Terraces

Begin your day at sunrise at the top of the Mammoth Terraces. Enter the Upper Terrace Road and park at the first parking area on the right. Walk down the boardwalk and out onto the terraces. From this point, the sun rises directly in front of you, but there is also often good color to the west just before the sun crests the horizon. Look for the dead trees on your left to add structure and interest to your composition. Continue walking straight ahead to the end of the boardwalk for sweeping views to the east and north. Watch for backlit steam filtering through the trees creating patterns of light rays. After the sun rises, concentrate on the colors and patterns in the thermal areas along the boardwalks.

◀2 Orange Mound Spring

Back in the car, continue along the one-way road to the parking area at Orange Mound Spring to photograph the colors and patterns in the formation. Then continue along the Upper Terrace Road and when it rejoins the main park road, turn left.

■3 Liberty Cap

Head back toward Mammoth and park at the lowest parking area in front of the formation known as Liberty Cap. Walk out onto the boardwalk to create images of the travertine formations and steamy backlit trees in the early morning light.

■4 Undine Falls

Turn right (east) at Mammoth Junction to follow the main park road to Tower Junction. Cross the high bridge over the Gardner River, and in approximately two miles, stop at the parking area on the left to photograph Undine Falls. Then continue on toward Tower Junction. In the area of Lava Creek, keep a watch for bull elk browsing in the meadows along the roadside, as well as small herds of bison.

▶5 Blacktail Deer Plateau Drive

(Optional drive, closed at night and in inclement weather)

After leaving Undine Falls, in approximately 4 miles, depending on the season and road conditions, turn right onto the Blacktail Plateau Drive. This 7-mile, one-way dirt road (not suitable for all cars) parallels the main road and offers sweeping views and meadows of wildflowers in July and early August.

▪6 Calcite Springs

At Tower Junction, continue straight ahead on the main park road and up the hill to Calcite Springs. Walk the boardwalk here for magnificent views of the end of the Grand Canyon of the Yellowstone and the basalt columns along the canyon. Look for ospreys and their nests on the canyon walls. Additional pullouts as you continue on the road to Tower Fall offer scenic vistas of the basalt columns, the canyon walls, and the Yellowstone River below. At the Tower Fall parking area, it is a short walk to the overlook to view and photograph this graceful 132-foot waterfall.

▶7 Mount Washburn

Leaving Tower Fall, turn left toward Canyon Junction. As you climb up Mount Washburn, there will be small parking areas on your left with spectacular vistas across Antelope Valley to the Absaroka Mountains in the distance. From late June to early August, the meadows on the west side of the road are carpeted with wildflowers. Keep in mind that the areas both above and below the road are grizzly bear management areas and are closed to entry, so please respect the signs that mark the closed areas.

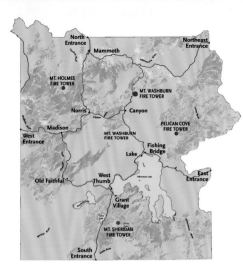

The orange and yellow areas show the extent of the 1988 burn.

◄8 Remnants of the 1988 Fire

Just after the two switchback curves, stop at the parking area on the right for views of the remnants of the fires that swept through this area in August and September of 1988. Use a long lens to capture dramatic images of the patterns and lines of the burned trees.

■9 Meadows on Dunraven Pass

Enjoy sweeping vistas as you cross Dunraven Pass and head toward Canyon Junction. Just after you begin the descent from the pass, stop at the parking area on your left to photograph the scenery. During midsummer, meadows of wildflowers color both sides of the road with as many as fifteen species blooming at once. Please do not pick or trample these plants, which are extremely fragile and must survive harsh conditions and a very short growing season.

■10 Lookout Point

At Canyon Junction, continue straight ahead to access both the north and south rims of the Grand Canyon of the Yellowstone and to photograph the spectacular canyon and the upper and lower falls. Approximately 1½ miles south of Canyon Junction, turn left onto North Rim Drive. Lookout Point is excellent for photographing the canyon and Lower Falls. In late morning, a rainbow often forms in the mist behind the falls. Lookout Point is also a good place to search for ospreys that nest on the canyon walls. Take a wide-angle lens for photographing the canyon, and a longer lens for capturing the colors and patterns of the canyon walls and Lower Falls. Grandview and Inspiration Points provide spectacular views of the canyon in both directions.

For an optional, strenuous hike, take the Red Rock Point Trail. The trailhead is just a few yards after the beginning of the paved walk to Lookout Point. Take the path to the right down to Red Rock Point for an intimate view of the Lower Falls. Bring a plastic grocery bag to protect your camera from mist, especially on windy days. As you descend the trail, be certain that you are in shape to make the climb back up, remembering that you are at an altitude of nearly 8,000 feet. Allow 1 hour for this hike and be sure to take water.

Insider's Tip

If you're using a tripod, don't block the boardwalks. Be aware of bouncing boardwalks, and watch for running children.

■11 Artist Point

Approximately 2 miles south of Canyon Junction, turn left to access the viewpoints first for Upper Falls and then for Artist Point. As you walk from the parking area to Artist Point, look to the left for views of the canyon and Lower Falls. Late afternoon sun provides dramatic lighting and colors on the canyon walls as you look toward the falls from this area. Continue on to both the upper and lower viewpoints at Artist Point.

▼12 Porcelain Basin

Return to Canyon Junction and turn left (west) toward Norris Junction. Watch for bull elk grazing in the Canyon Meadows. At Norris Junction, continue straight into the parking area for Norris Geyser Basin. After entering the basin, turn right when the path forks, walk through the Norris Museum, and take the path down into Porcelain Basin. Here you can photograph the many colors and patterns of the thermal features along the edges of the boardwalk. There are also several small geysers that erupt frequently. Take a wide-angle lens for scenic shots and a macro lens for close-up photographs. Before reaching the basin, take the spur loop trail on your right, which provides a vantage point for an overview of the basin and closer access to several colorful pools.

Photographing in Porcelain Basin is very rewarding in late afternoon and evening light, especially if there are clouds in the sky. Perpetual steam clouds around Ledge Geyser (along the trail down into the basin) can produce spectacular images when shooting the sunset facing west, or facing south from lower in the basin. Don't forget to also check the sky to the east.

All photographs in this chapter by the section's author, Sandra Nykerk.

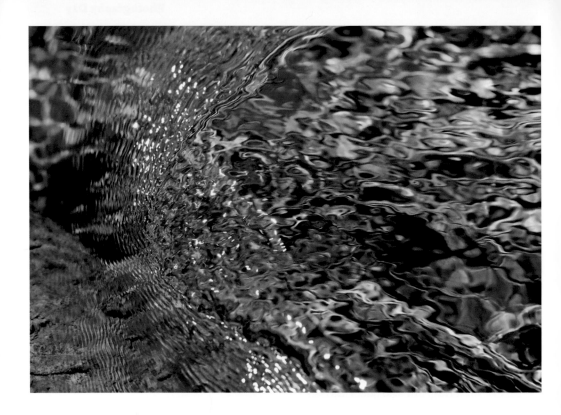

■13 The Back Basin (optional hike)

Return to the museum and continue straight on the trail that heads south into the Back Basin. Along the way, stop at the photogenic Emerald Pool on the right, then Steamboat Geyser, which erupts very infrequently, on the left. At the bottom of the steps, turn right and continue to Cistern Spring. There is an overlook on the boardwalk where you can photograph this beautiful spring, or continue a few more yards and photograph the colorful terraces through the dramatic trees burned in the fires of 1988. Retrace your steps to return to the parking area, or continue ahead on the loop trail to return to the museum.

▲14 Swan Lake Flats

Leave Norris Geyser Basin and turn left (north) at Norris Junction. Watch for elk and bison in Norris Meadows, and look for how the late afternoon and evening light can produce dramatic scenics across the meadows and along the Gibbon River. Continue toward Mammoth Hot Springs, passing North and South Twin Lakes and Roaring Mountain. Continue on to Swan Lake Flats for sunset.

Sunset is an excellent time to photograph the landscape. At Swan Lake Flats, park at the second parking area on the left. From here, you will have a western viewpoint of the meadows and the Gallatin Range, as well as the magnificent Electric Peak. There are also sweeping views to the east. If it is calm, take the path out to Swan Lake to photograph the reflection of Electric Peak and any clouds in the sky. Watch for bison and be aware that this area is frequented by both black and grizzly bears, so stay alert and take your bear spray.

Insider's Tip

WARNING! The spray from the geysers can ruin your lenses!

Insider's Tip

If your youthful visitors are interested in earning a Jr. Ranger badge, get the brochure in advance so that you can go over it with them so they know what to expect.

Young scientist booklets are available for purchase at the Old Faithful Visitor Education Center and the Canyon Visitor Education Center.

Things to Bring

Save time, frustration, and energy by being prepared.

- A cooler with snacks, drinks, lunch, and treats

- Field guides and wildlife checklists

- Binoculars, magnifying glass, and anything that can enhance the experience

Kid's Day

Madison Information Station to Canyon Visitor Education Center

Yellowstone for children isn't about rushing around and checking sites off the list.

It's about experiencing the park on a sensory level with an educational focus. You can't rush children. It is the sights, the smells, the sounds, and the tactile experiences they will remember. Each child is different and has different ways of learning. Give them a gift of a day in letting them lead down the path of what they are interested in. Even if you only manage to experience two or three activities in a day, it is a success if the child is able to enjoy those activities on their own.

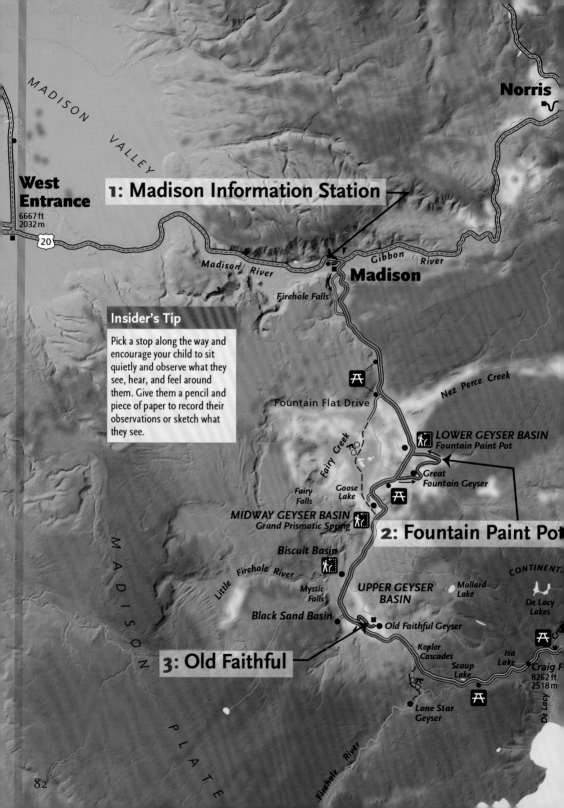

Norris

West Entrance
6667 ft
2032 m

20

MADISON VALLEY

Madison River

Gibbon River

1: Madison Information Station

Madison

Firehole Falls

Insider's Tip

Pick a stop along the way and encourage your child to sit quietly and observe what they see, hear, and feel around them. Give them a pencil and piece of paper to record their observations or sketch what they see.

Fountain Flat Drive

Nez Perce Creek

Fairy Creek

LOWER GEYSER BASIN
Fountain Paint Pot

Great Fountain Geyser

Fairy Falls

Goose Lake

MIDWAY GEYSER BASIN
Grand Prismatic Spring

2: Fountain Paint Pot

Biscuit Basin

Little Firehole River

UPPER GEYSER BASIN

Mallard Lake

CONTINENT

De Lacy Lakes

Mystic Falls

Black Sand Basin

Old Faithful Geyser

3: Old Faithful

Kepler Cascades

Isa Lake

Scaup Lake

Craig
8262 ft
2518 m

De Lacy Cr

Lone Star Geyser

MADISON PLATEAU

Firehole River

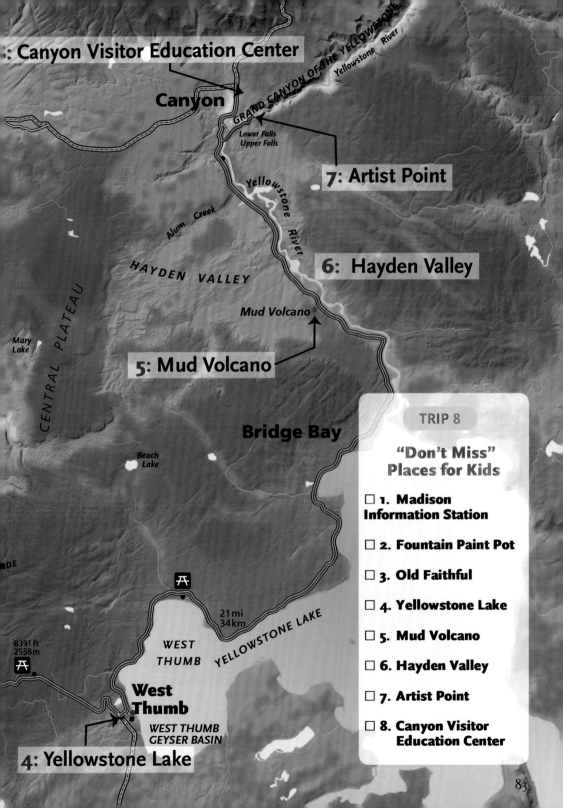

8: Canyon Visitor Education Center

Canyon

GRAND CANYON OF THE YELLOWSTONE

Yellowstone River

Lower Falls
Upper Falls

Yellowstone River

7: Artist Point

Alum. Creek

HAYDEN VALLEY

6: Hayden Valley

Mud Volcano

5: Mud Volcano

Mary Lake

CENTRAL PLATEAU

Bridge Bay

Beach Lake

21 mi
34 km

WEST THUMB

YELLOWSTONE LAKE

8391 ft
2558 m

West Thumb

WEST THUMB GEYSER BASIN

4: Yellowstone Lake

Stops to Interest the Young Visitor

▪1 Madison Information Station

Start your day at the Junior Ranger Station at the Madison Information Station. Pick up a Junior Ranger activity book, but keep in mind that the Junior Ranger program can take more than one day to complete and that it requires attending one of the free ranger programs held in the park. While at Madison, visit the touch table for kids and consider watching one of the 30-minute programs that run daily during the summer. Also check out the eruption prediction for Old Faithful and try to time your arrival to Upper Geyser Basin accordingly.

> **Fun Fact:**
>
> Madison Junction is where the Gibbon and Firehole rivers converge into the Madison River. Meriwether Lewis, of the Lewis and Clark expedition, named the Madison River in 1805 for then U.S. Secretary of State James Madison.

▪2 Fountain Paint Pot

Kids love the blooping sounds and bubbling appearance of mudpots. Enjoy this easy, ½-mile loop walk (suitable for all ages) that passes all four kinds of thermal features: fumaroles, geysers, hot springs, and mudpots. This walk provides a sensory experience with wonderful sights, interesting smells, and foggy steam to walk through and feel.

▪3 Old Faithful

Before or after watching Old Faithful erupt, visit the Young Scientist room at the Old Faithful Visitor Education Center. The interactive exhibits, designed just for kids, are least busy right before and during eruptions, or in early morning and early evening. Walk the ¾-mile loop around Old Faithful Geyser to get a different point of view.

Photo by Birdiegal717, dreamstime

Wildlife

Children especially love Yellowstone's wildlife. Kids can be great at reminding their parents of park safety regulations concerning wildlife.

1. Stay at least 100 yards away from wolves and bears and stay at least 25 yards away from all other animals.

2. Don't feed any park animals, including bears, coyotes, ground squirrels, chipmunks, and ravens.

3. Stop in pullouts, not in the middle of the road blocking other vehicles.

4. Hike in groups. Make noise so bears and other animals aren't startled. Carry bear spray and know how to use it. If you encounter a bear, do NOT run.

5. Keep a clean camp. Store food and scented items in vehicles, not in tents. Follow all regulations posted in each park campground.

84

■4 Yellowstone Lake

From Old Faithful, head southeast toward West Thumb Junction. At the junction turn left and head toward Fishing Bridge.

Along the lake there are many good places to stop and have a picnic lunch and play in the sand and dip your feet in the water. One of our favorites is Gull Point Drive. Gray jays often call and beg for a handout, so be on guard with keeping food items secure and of course, no feeding wildlife! This is a good time for working on the Junior Ranger booklet. After lunch, store all food items and walk down to the shore. Kids love throwing rocks into the lake, building pretend houses or forts with driftwood, and finding shiny pieces of obsidian in the sand. This is a great place to fish from the shore if you have a permit. Consider a stop at the Fishing Bridge store for ice cream.

■5 Mud Volcano

Follow the Yellowstone River north and stop at Mud Volcano. This area always produces funny smells, like rotten eggs, due to hydrogen sulfide gas. Some kids love it because it's stinky. Also check out Sulphur Caldron on the opposite (east) side of the road.

■6 Hayden Valley

Continue north through Hayden Valley. This is one of the best places to see bison in the park. Take time to stop at one of the pullouts and familiarize your children with the use of binoculars. There is often plenty of large wildlife to observe, but even if you don't see any animals, a great activity is to just sit and learn to look. It will amaze you and your children to see what slowly comes into view...a pair of mallards, an osprey flying overhead, a bald eagle, or maybe a ground squirrel poking up its head and looking at you!

■7 Artist Point

Don't miss this stop! The view of the canyon and the size, sound, and spray of the waterfall amaze children. This is another good place to use those binoculars. Look for nesting ospreys along the canyon walls.

■8 Canyon Visitor Education Center

If your children completed a Junior Ranger booklet, stop at the Canyon Visitor Education Center for a ranger to check over the paper and award the badge. This is a proud moment for not only the child, but for the parents as well. Also check out the exhibits.

Fun Fact:

Yellowstone Lake is the largest high-elevation lake in North America. It is 20 miles long by 14 miles wide.

Fun Fact:

The hump on a bison's back is made of muscle that enables the animal to use its head to plow through snow during the winter months.

Fun Fact:

Around 50 million bison likely roamed this area and the Great Plains before the 1800s. Today, Yellowstone's two herds, each with thousands of individuals, form the largest population of bison on public land.

Photo by Varina And Jay Patel, dreamstime

Fishing Day

Gardner River to Trout Lake

Considered one of the premier fly fishing destinations in the world, Yellowstone National Park boasts thousands of miles of rivers and streams and hundreds of lakes and ponds, almost all filled with fish.

With so many options to choose from, it can be hard to decide where to focus your time. In one trip to the park you could fish the 132-square-mile Yellowstone Lake, the thermal heated waters of the Firehole River, and a backcountry stream like Cache Creek. While it would take a lifetime to fish all the park's waters, that doesn't mean that if you only have 24 hours to wet a line you can't experience some of the great angling. This itinerary describes some of the fishing options that could be covered in one day on Yellowstone's Northern Range, from the North Entrance to the Northeast Entrance. Of course, if you find a beautiful stretch of water where the fish are biting, feel free to throw the plan out the window and stay where you are.

Gardiner
North Entrance
5314 ft
1620 m

Park Headquarters

Yellowstone

1: Gardner River

Blacktail
Pond

Mammoth-Tower Road

Undine
Falls

Wraith
Falls

River

Blacktail Plateau Drive

one-way

*BLACKTAIL DEER
PLATEAU*

18 mi
29 km

Floating
Island
Lake

3: Slough

Tower-Roosevelt
6270 ft
1911 m

Petrified Tree

Gardner River

Swan
Lake

one-way

2: Yellowstone River

Prospect Peak
9525 ft
2903 m

21 mi
34 km

Tower

Creek

Lava Creek

Chittenden
Road

Antelope Creek

Beaver
Lake

● Obsidian Cliff
7383 ft
2250 m

Mount Washbur
10243 ft
3122 m

Grizzly
Lake

TRIP 9

Gardner River to Trout Lake

☐ **1. Gardner River**

☐ **2. Yellowstone River**

☐ **3. Slough Creek**

☐ **4. Lamar River**

☐ **5. Soda Butte Creek**

☐ **6. Cache Creek**

☐ **7. Trout Lake**

12 mi
19 km

*Lower Falls
Upper Falls*

Yellowstone

GRAND CANY

Alum Creek

Slough Creek △

212

Northeast Entrance
7365 ft
2245 m

Barrone
10004 ft
3171 m

Abiathar
Peak
10928 m

🏕

Pebble
Creek

7: Trout Lake

△

Trout
Lake

Cache Mountain
9596 ft
2925 m

Yellowstone
Association
Institute

LAMAR VALLEY

Soda Butte Creek

Lamar River

29 mi
47 km

🚶

Mount
Norris
9936 ft
3028 m

Cache Creek

5: Soda Butte Creek

Lamar River Trail to Cache Creek Trail

Lamar River

6: Cache Creek

MIRROR PLATEAU

◀1 Gardner River

A classic mountain stream, most of the fishing on the Gardner is focused on the stretch from the High Bridge on the Mammoth-Tower road down to the confluence with the Yellowstone River. Home to a variety of trout and a wide range of sizes, this river features a plethora of fishing opportunities. There is swift moving pocket water, long riffles, and open meadows, all which can be searched with attractor patterns, classic nymphs like princes and stoneflies, and streamers. Golden stones and salmonflies can attract rising fish, as can high-floating terrestrials.

▼2 Yellowstone River

The longest undammed river in the lower 48 states feeds into, and then flows out of, Yellowstone Lake, home to the world's largest genetically pure population of Yellowstone cutthroat. While these native trout can be found upstream of the Grand Canyon of the Yellowstone, other sections of this river, below the canyon, are also home to brown, brook, and rainbow trout, as well as mountain whitefish, making it a great place to try to catch as many different species as possible. The hatches on the Yellowstone are almost too many to count so it pays to be prepared for anything, though early in the morning keep an eye out for drakes, pale morning duns, and sedge caddisflies.

Special Considerations

A Yellowstone fishing permit is needed for all anglers 16 years of age or older. Children under 15 may receive a free permit signed by an adult or fish without a permit if accompanied by an adult with a valid permit.

Photo by Pat Clayton

■3 Slough Creek

For those looking to get away from the road, Slough Creek offers some of park's best (and most challenging) fishing in a setting that is pure Yellowstone beauty. People talking about the world-famous fishing on Slough usually break down their discussion into meadows, the open areas on the river that can be reached from the trail that leaves the parking lot near the Slough Creek campground. The first meadow is about a one hour hike, the second about two hours, and the third about three. In each meadow, you'll find wary cutthroats—some over 20 inches—in slow, crystal clear water. Be it *Baetis*, pale morning duns, terrestrials or the ever-present midges, even if you match what these easy-to-see trout are eating, they can be very hard to catch.

Planning Ahead

No special reservations are necessary, though you will need to purchase a Yellowstone fishing permit at a ranger station, visitor center, park general store, or fly shop outside the park.

In order to make the most of your trip, check fishing reports before you travel to the park since certain parts of the park are closed or are not fishable during certain times of the year. Be sure to review the park fishing regulations that are provided with your permit.

Things to Bring

Photo by Edward Fielding

- Fly rod outfit in the 4- to 6-wt. range.
- Waders/wading shoes
- Sunhat/sunscreen
- Yellowstone fishing permit
- Bear spray
- Picnic lunch and water
- Flies/tackle

Insider's Tip

Since the discovery of nonnative lake trout in Yellowstone Lake in the 1990s, the park's population of Yellowstone cutthroat has been imperiled. Though the National Park Service is doing everything in their power to eradicate lake trout and other invasive species that threaten to outcompete or interbreed with native species, it is important that anglers follow all park rules and regulations to protect the park's fish and fisheries. For more information about the issues facing Yellowstone fisheries, visit: nps.gov/yell/naturescience/fisheries_issues.htm

▲4 Lamar River

The Lamar River is easy to access because it follows the North Entrance road through Lamar Valley and parking is available in any of the pullouts that line the road. Since the river mostly meanders through open terrain that is home to bison, elk, pronghorn, and even grizzlies and wolves, it has very little structure, meaning it can be hard to find where the fish will be holding from one day to the next. Still, during the warmth of the day, fishing with flies that mimic large terrestrials, like grasshoppers, ants, beetles, and crickets, close to undercut banks and along seams in the current can produce rises from cutthroats as well as the small population of rainbows that inhabit the river.

▪5 Soda Butte Creek

Soda Butte Creek enters the Lamar River from the northeast. These two waterways converge at "the confluence," a heavily fished area thanks to its deep pools and convenient location right across from the Lamar River Stock Trailhead. In fact, with its

Regulations

Anglers must follow all of the NPS rules outlined in the park's fishing regulations, including:

- Only using lead-free, artificial lures and flies with barbless hooks.

- Bait is prohibited.

- All cutthroat trout, mountain whitefish and Arctic grayling must be released unharmed.

- Remove nonnative fish where they harm cutthroat trout. There are no limits on nonnatives in the Native Trout Conservation Area.

- All lake trout in Yellowstone Lake must be killed.

- All rainbow and brook trout in the Lamar River drainage, including Slough Creek and Soda Butte Creeks, must be killed.

Yellowstone
Cutthroat Trout

During spring, runoff produced from melting snow makes many of the park's waters unfishable. But don't worry; the months of May and June are the perfect time of year to experience the waters of the Firehole and Madison rivers, which become too hot to fish during the summer months. Heated by the thermal features in the Old Faithful area, the Firehole has daily hatches of pale morning duns, blue-winged olives, and a variety of caddisflies. The technical waters of the Madison can be tricky for beginners but this world-renowned trout stream offers anglers the chance to cast to rising fish, especially during the early-June salmonfly hatch. During the fall, these two rivers again provide great fishing opportunities, most notably the Madison, which sees an influx of trophy brown and rainbow trout that enter the river to spawn.

proximity to the road, manageable size (you can jump across it in some places) and predictable pocket water, Soda Butte is one of the busiest rivers in the park. But despite the crowds, anglers that are willing to walk a little bit can often find 10- to 14-inch cutthroats, as well as the rare fish pushing 16 inches, rising to pale morning duns or, during hot days, gulping terrestrials like beetles and ants.

◼6 Cache Creek

Cache Creek is a backcountry stream that can be reached by parking at the Soda Butte/Lamar River Trailhead, just past the Lamar River Stock Trailhead, and following the Lamar River Trail for three miles until you encounter the creek. Most anglers fish upstream, targeting rising fish as they go with mayfly patterns as well as terrestrials. Though this water gets a fair bit of pressure from pack trips, this is still a remote area of the park that is home to grizzly bears and wolves, so be sure to bring a friend and make a lot of noise as you fish.

▼7 Trout Lake

Less than a mile hike from the road, the 12-acre Trout Lake is home to some the largest cutthroat and rainbow trout in Yellowstone National Park. Much like Slough Creek, the fish are easy to see here but it takes skill to land them. Anglers that have the most luck here often fish below the surface with damselfly nymphs, scuds, soft hackles, worms, and streamers like woolly buggers and leeches. In the evening, *Callibaetis* hatches can produce rising fish, as can terrestrials, but presentation and light leaders are key to drawing the interest of the much-fished trout.

Photo by Slouder, dreamstime

To create this guide, we gathered the thoughts and plans of local area experts and park employees. They suggested routes and stops so you see the best of what Yellowstone has to offer in a limited amount of time.

Our expert contributors:

Katy Duffy is an ecologist, an education ranger, and a well-known birder at Yellowstone National Park. She can identify raptors on the wing and songbirds by sound. *(Birding Day, page 48)*

Carolyn Harwood is an interpreter and resident instructor for the Yellowstone Association Institute. She has hiked more than 2,000 miles in Yellowstone. *(Wildlife and Geology days, pages 36 and 56)*

Sandra Nykerk teaches photography and natural history programs and exhibits her art around the West. *(Photography Day, page 70)*

Kathy Russell is an educator and has worked seasonally in Yellowstone for more than 20 years. *(Kid's Day, page 80)*

Bob Fuhrmann is the Education Program Director for Yellowstone National Park. *(Kid's Day, page 80)*

Stephen Camelio is an award-winning writer and the former research editor for *In Style* special magazines. He lives on the Yellowstone River in Gardiner, Montana. *(Fishing Day, page 86)*